CW00550749

To Tom T...

With APPRECIATION
FROM
Tom E...

VISION TITLES PUBLISHING

90 DAYS DEVOTIONAL

 Complete with

DAILY

PRAYERS

BIBLE PASSAGES

AND

JOURNAL

FOR MEN & WOMEN

VOL. 1

Also By Ademola Borode

FROM DREAMS TO DELIVERANCE

"Strange dreams, Meanings, Specific Psalms and Acidic Prayer Points That Triggers Divine Solutions"

THAT'S NOT HIS FAULT

"A Down To Earth Approach for Purposeful Living"

90 DAYS DEVOTIONAL WITH DAILY PRAYERS FOR MEN AND WOMEN

"A 15 minutes daily spiritual workout with Jesus"

(*Devotional only*)

Also available on Amazon and https://ademolaborode.org

ADEMOLA BORODE

90 DAYS
DEVOTIONAL

Complete with
DAILY
PRAYERS
BIBLE PASSAGES
AND
JOURNAL
FOR MEN & WOMEN

VOL. 1

A 15 MINUTE DAILY SPIRITUAL
WORKOUT WITH JESUS

VISION TITLES PUBLISHING
OWINGS MILLS, USA MARYLAND 21117

We want to hear from you. Please send your comments about this book to us at
VISIONTITLES@OUTLOOK.COM
TJNIKE2002@HOTMAIL.COM

OWINGS MILLS, MARYLAND 21117 USA

90 DAYS DEVOTIONAL
Copyright © 2020 by Ademola Borode
ISBN: 978-1-7353942-3-7

Requests for Information should be addressed to:
Visiontitles@outlook.com

Also, visit our website at https://ademolaborode.org

Cover and Interior design by Vision Titles Publishing
Printed in the United States of America

Specially Dedicated to all those people all over the world who know they are not perfect but continually strive towards perfection every day of their lives and to all those who desire to live victoriously over the devil and his agents in every area of their lives.

Most importantly, To the Almighty God, the Alpha and Omega, for giving me the divine inspiration to write, the determination and the will power to sit for those long hours to put this daily devotional and Journal together to be available for you, the reader, and also for posterity.

CONTENTS

MY COMMITMENT

With God's divine assistance, I commit at least 15 minutes of each day of the next 90 days of my life to faithfully seek Gods face, study his word and reflect upon everything I'm devoting my time to study in this book. In Jesus Name.

So, help me God.

_____

YOUR NAME

_____

YOUR PARTNER'S NAME

Ademola Borode

_____

ADEMOLA BORODE PhD

_____

TODAY'S DATE

DAY 1
YOU ARE ON A MISSION
James 1:16-18
MEMORY VERSE

Of his own will He brought us forth by the word of truth, that we might be a kind of first fruits of His creatures. James 1:18 Nkjv

EXPOSITION

Yes! You are here on a mission and that's for a fact, just in case you're still wondering what you are here for. God has created you for a purpose, therefore, you are not on earth by accident or by happenstance. So, you have to desire for that purpose why you were created, to be fulfilled otherwise you would have passed through this earth for nothing without making an impact. You don't want to live like Methuselah whose only record was that "He lived, and He Died".

In fulfilling your mission here, you cannot afford to leave the God who has sent you on that mission out of the journey, otherwise, your stay here would just be a waste. That's why it's very important to daily commit your ways into the hands of the lord and ask him for guidance and direction before you head out on your daily endeavors.

It's not proper if you just continue to live in oblivion without even asking him what he has sent you here to do. This is because, those who have discovered why they are here, are those who end up being celebrated in their lifetime and even long after they are dead. The bible says: Many are the plans in a person's heart, but it is the Lord's purpose that prevails. (Proverbs 19:21). Ask the lord about your mission here and he'll guide you aright.

PRAYERS FOR THE DAY

*My father and my God reveal your purpose for my life unto me today in the name of Jesus.

*I shall fulfill my divine purpose on earth in the name of Jesus.

EXTRA RESOURCES FOR READING
Jeremiah 1:4-10, Proverbs 19:20-23

Giving Thanks for:---

I'm Praying for:--

Devotional Reflections On My Heart Today :--

Things I'm Still Struggling With :--

-------------------------   ---
-- --

DAY 2
LIVING FOR CHRIST EVERY DAY
Romans 12:1-8
MEMORY VERSE
"Do not conform to the pattern of this world but be transformed by the renewing of your mind. Then you will be able to test and approve what God's will is—his good, pleasing and perfect will. Romans 12:2 Niv"

EXPOSITION
In our sojourn on planet earth as Christians who desire to go to a perfect heaven, we need to realize that we must endeavor to live a perfectly holy life that is without blame or reproach of any sort. This is because we have a God and father who cannot allow any form of impurity to come near him or his domain. The bible says God is of purer eyes than to behold iniquity (Habakkuk 1:13).

There are various forms of distractions that compete for God's attention in our lives every day and these distractions often come in forms of evil thoughts and ideas which when not quickly discarded or tossed out usually transform into actions and those actions eventually becomes character. For this reason, we are admonished by Apostle Paul in the memory verse above to renew our minds.

How can we renew our minds if not through meditation on the words of God daily? That way we would begin to understand the mind of God concerning us and what he expects from us and how he wants us to live our lives, so as to be able to reflect his glory. That way we are transformed from within and those we come in contact with, would know that truly we are his disciples. May you be found qualified as a vessel unto honor in the name of Jesus.

PRAYERS FOR THE DAY
*Lord transform my life, by your power into the person you want me to be, that I may bring glory unto your name, in Jesus name.

*Lord empower me to live for you every day in Jesus Name.

EXTRA RESOURCES FOR READING
Romans 14:7-12., Romans 12:1-8., Mathew 7:21-23

Giving Thanks for:--

I'm Praying for:--

Devotional Reflections On My Heart Today :--

Things I'm Still Struggling With :--

DAY 3
CHANGE THE BATTLEGROUND!!!
2 Chronicles 20: 15-17
MEMORY VERSE
"Do not be afraid or discouraged because of this vast army. For the battle is not yours, but God's. II Chronicles20:17"

EXPOSITION

On Several occasions in the scriptures, we see God talking to his people in this way, when they are facing a potential challenge and it seems as if they are intimidated. As Christians of this age, when the enemy comes calling with the challenges of life, and it seems you are being intimidated, all we need to do is just take the battle to the lord in prayers. Take it out of the physical realm into the spiritual realm.

Let, take an Eagle for example. When an eagle goes hunting, it spots a deadly snake in its comfort zone on land, the Eagle never gets intimidated by the dangers or potential risk of engaging the serpent. All it does is to pick up the serpent and change the battleground. The Eagle takes the potentially dangerous prey off the ground and takes it up into the heavenlies where the snake is powerless, and the eagle is at an advantage.

Likewise, as children of God, when you learn to change the battle ground, victory is sure. Go on your knees in prayers because those who win the battle of life do so on their knees. "Anyone who kneels before God in prayers would stand before any situation ". In the passage above, King Jehoshaphat changed the battle ground for the enemy, he went to God in prayers and the lord appeared in an uncommon way and victory was secured. Prayer changes things!!

PRAYERS FOR THE DAY:
*Oh lord arise and show yourself mighty in my battles in the name of Jesus.

* I refuse to be defeated in the battle of life in the name of Jesus.

EXTRA RESOURCES FOR READING
Exodus 14:13-14., Isaiah 41:10., Deut. 1: 29-30.

Giving Thanks for:--

I'm Praying for:---

Devotional Reflections On My Heart Today :------------------------------------
----

Things I'm Still Struggling With :--

DAY 4
THE POWER OF RESURRECTION
Philippians 3:10-21.
MEMORY VERSE
'That I may know him, and the power of his resurrection and the fellowship of his sufferings being made conformable unto his death. Philippians 3:10."

EXPOSITION
Apostle Paul said in this Passage here, that I may know him and the power of his resurrection. This power of resurrection is the main thing that every child of God needs to come in contact with. Because many people have not yet experienced the power, that's the reason why the enemy is still toying with many so-called believers, Pastors, Preachers, Bishops and church goers in this Generation.

When this power comes on you, your spirit man becomes supercharged with fire. When the Apostles encountered the power at Pentecost, they turned the whole world upside down for Jesus. When our founding fathers of the Christian faith encountered the power, they emptied Hospitals of patients, medical personnels had less to do, because no more sick people were available for treatment because of the visitation of the Power of resurrection.

In John 11:25, this personality called the resurrection power spoke there. He told Martha "I am the resurrection and the life". When the resurrection power locates you, every negative situation immediately transforms into positive, every dead situation automatically receives life. That power is the Lord Jesus Christ himself who captured death in victory. I pray for you that you will experience that power of resurrection this very day in the mighty name of Jesus.

PRAYERS FOR THE DAY
*Every good thing that is dead in my life, let the power of resurrection bring them back to life today in the Name of Jesus.

*Resurrection power do wonders in my life today in Jesus name.

EXTRA RESOURCES FOR READING
John 11:17-44., 1 Peter 1:3-9., Philippians 3:10-21

Giving Thanks for:---

I'm Praying for:---

Devotional Reflections On My Heart Today :-----------------------------------

----

Things I'm Still Struggling With :---

------------------------   --

DAY 5
WHO ARE YOU?
1 Peter 2: 9-12
MEMORY VERSE

"But you are a chosen people, a royal priesthood, a holy nation, God's special possession, that you may declare the praises of him who called you out of darkness into his wonderful light. 1 Peter 2:9 (Niv)"

EXPOSITION

One of the most dangerous things that can ever happen to a person is if that person does not know who he or she is. When a prince does not know that he is a prince, even a slave in the palace would take him for a ride and nothing in form of repercussion would happen to that slave. However, the very day the prince knows that he is the heir to the throne, then that day marks the end of his insults.

I once heard about an age long fairy tale about a farmer who brought home an egg he found somewhere on his farm. So, he added that egg to the batch of eggs his hen was laying. The hen incubated the eggs and they all hatched later. As they all grew together, this tiny chick always sees an eagle flying over and realized that she looks more like that eagle in the sky and the clucking sound of that eagle sounds more like its own.

So, one day it stretched its wings and flapped and up in the sky it went. From that day forward it never came back to the rest of the chicks because it now knows that it doesn't belong there. Beloved, you need to know who you are, and who you are made of, otherwise the devil would cheat you. May you receive insight today in Jesus Name.

PRAYERS FOR THE DAY

*Lord, help me to discover myself and my potentials in the name of Jesus.

*My true potentials come alive by the power in the name of Jesus.

EXTRA RESOURCES FOR READING
Hosea 4:6a., Psalms 139:13-16., Isaiah 62:3-5

Giving Thanks for:---

I'm Praying for:--

Devotional Reflections On My Heart Today :-----------------------------------
----

Things I'm Still Struggling With :---

DAY 6
YOU CAN BE BETTER THAN THIS
Jeremiah 29:11-14
MEMORY VERSE
"For I know the plans I have for you," declares the Lord, "plans to prosper you and not to harm you, plans to give you hope and a future. Jeremiah 29:11(Niv)"

EXPOSITION
The desire of our lord is to see each and every one of us, his subjects to grow into better people, so we can, by the manifestation of his goodness in our lives, bring more people into his kingdom. That's why that passage above is telling us in very clear terms how God wants us to live in abundance of everything here on earth. It is however sad, that lots of Christians are still living below that God's set plan.

If our God so much wants us to prosper in every way, then we need to always strive to do our best to live in accordance with his word so that we do not give the devil a chance in our lives, thereby putting a wedge in our relationship with the lord which definitely would close the way to our being able to prosper God's way.

Irrespective of whichever point or level you are currently in your Christian walk, you have to know that you can still be better if you strive continuously towards perfection. It doesn't matter whatever your background is as a person, you can rise up from that level and become a much better person to the glory of the lord if you continuously work at it and keep fighting the good fight and with the help of God, if you do not rely only on your own power and strength, you would get there.

PRAYERS FOR THE DAY
*Oh Lord my God, empower me to strive towards perfection every day, so I can be better than this in Jesus Name.

*Root of imperfection in my life, wither and die in Jesus Name.
EXTRA RESOURCES FOR READING
1 Corinthians 9:24-27., Jeremiah 29:11-14., Philippians 4:6-8

Giving Thanks for:---

I'm Praying for:--

Devotional Reflections On My Heart Today :------------------------------------
----

Things I'm Still Struggling With :---

DAY 7
WHAT DOES GOD EXPECT OF ME?
Micah 6:6-9
MEMORY VERSE

He has shown you, O mortal, what is good. And what does the Lord require of you? To act justly and to love mercy and to walk humbly with your God. Micah 6:8 (Niv)

EXPOSITION!

Our God is a God of fairness and justice in whom there is no guile or iniquity and he expects us, as his children on earth to act justly and to walk without any blame or reproach before him at all times. The lord wants us to walk in humility before God and to always show mercy to others.

One of the things which the lord hates to see in the life of any believer is Pride. That is why he told us through his word that He resists the Proud but gives grace to the humble. James 4:6. If he would abide with us and not apart from us, then the sin of Pride must be dealt with decisively and instead put on humility just as Jesus was humble even unto death.

I used to know a brother back in the days who said to me one day that "I know I am a proud person and I am proud of it". Imagine a Christian boasting of the sin of Pride? But do you know that brother is not alone in that, because there are many in the Christian fold who are in the same situation and are not doing anything about it to get themselves delivered from that Sin.

As children of God, we must ask God to help us to die to self so we can bear fruits unto righteousness like Apostle Paul said about Himself that "I die daily". 1 Corinthians 15:31

PRAYERS FOR THE DAY

*Lord give me grace and empower me to die to self in Jesus Name

*Every weakness in my spirit man that the enemy want to use to send me to hell, release me now in the Name of Jesus.

EXTRA RESOURCES FOR READING
Proverbs 29:19-23., Philippians 2:1-11.

Giving Thanks for:--

I'm Praying for:---

Devotional Reflections On My Heart Today :----------------------------------
----

Things I'm Still Struggling With :--

DAY 8
LET GOD ARISE
Psalm 68:1-6
MEMORY VERSE
Let God arise, Let His enemies be scattered; Let those also who hate Him flee before Him Psalm 68:1 (Nkjv)

EXPOSITION!

I've heard a few people say to my hearing in times past that they never offend anyone, and no one offends them, so they do not have enemies. Hmnn? How wrong can someone be that's beyond this kind of assertion. If you are among those who have that kind of notion, well I've got news for you.

The Devil is your number one enemy and all his demons are also included on that enemy list also. That's why the psalmist says in the memory verse above that let God arise and let his enemies be scattered. Anything that limits your potentials in the course of your earthly existence, is an enemy. If sickness limits your potentials, then it is an enemy you must fight. If poverty or lack of the right helper is limiting you then you have just discovered another enemy you have.

Whatever the lord has not created with you that keeps you from operating or living to your full capacity is your enemy and it is time for you to call upon the God of Israel, the alpha and omega now, to arise for your sake and scatter them before you in the name of Jesus. If you just cry out to the lord aggressively and sincerely, every situation that makes your life uncomfortable would scatter before your life in Jesus Name.

PRAYERS FOR THE DAY

*Oh God arise and destroy every enemy of my full-scale laughter scatter in the name of Jesus.

*Oh God deliver me from the grip of powers that are stronger than me in Jesus name.

EXTRA RESOURCES FOR READING
Psalm 94:1-2., Psalm 2:1-End., Psalm 3:1-8.

Giving Thanks for:---

I'm Praying for:--

Devotional Reflections On My Heart Today :------------------------------------
----

Things I'm Still Struggling With :---

DAY 9
I WILL LAUGH LAST
Luke 6:20-23
MEMORY VERSE

Blessed are you who hunger now, for you shall be filled.
Blessed are you who weep now, for you shall laugh.
Luke 6:21 (Nkjv)

EXPOSITION

It is no longer surprising to see children of God suffer in our world. As a matter of fact, that is part of the thing you signed up for the very minute you made up your mind to follow Christ, because Christ has not promised us a stress-free Christian journey. You could take a cue from the Apostles of old, some of whom even sacrificed their lives for the sake of the gospel.

Jesus said very clearly in the book of John 16:33 that you shall have tribulation in this world but that you should only rejoice because he has overcome the world. The very moment you choose to walk with Christ, you automatically become public enemy number one to the devil, so he would attempt to take away your joy, your dignity, your total well-being and even your very existence.

However, no matter how hard he tries to get you just like Job in the scriptures, if you do not compromise but stand your ground, you will laugh last because whoever laughs last laughs best. In the beatitudes from the sermon on the mount above, you could see Jesus telling you again there that though you may be weeping or hurting now, laughter and joy is coming your way. So, cheer up! Cast all your burdens upon him! There's so much light at the end of the tunnel.

PRAYERS FOR THE DAY

*Whether the devil likes it or not, my problems shall give up and I shall laugh last in the name of Jesus.

* By the power in the blood of Jesus, I am an overcomer in the name of Jesus.

EXTRA RESOURCES FOR READING
Genesis 21:1-7., Psalms 126:2-3

Giving Thanks for:---

I'm Praying for:---

Devotional Reflections On My Heart Today :---

Things I'm Still Struggling With :---

-------------------------- --

DAY 10
WHAT IS YOUR MINDSET
Philippians 4:4-9
MEMORY VERSE
Keep your heart with all diligence, for out of it spring
the issues of life. Proverbs 4:23 (Nkjv)
EXPOSITION!

As a Christian you need to know that you are whatever you think about all day. The bible admonishes us to think about the most edifying and honorable things every day because the mind is a terrible thing to waste. Positive and negative attitudes is a mindset and a reflection of your personal orientation to life.

No matter how much progress someone has seen in the past, it still doesn't stop a pessimistic mindset from exhibiting fear of defeat or failure especially if you surround yourself with people who have a negative outlook to life, then it would breath negative energy to influence you. If you always think about failure, then failures would always follow such a person around. If you always think about the possibility of things not working for you, then there's the likelihood of things not eventually working.

Maybe you have experienced some setbacks in the past, that doesn't mean you should now believe that's your lot and because you have a humble background doesn't mean that your back has to be on the ground in life. There are two ways to look at water inside a cup, it is either the cup is half filled or it is half empty. If you see it as half filled, then, there is still hope, but if you see it as half empty, then hope is lost. It about time you change your mindset!

PRAYERS FOR THE DAY

*Divine Power and ability to think positively about life always, fall upon my life in the name of Jesus.

*I take authority over every negative mindset and bring them to the obedience and control of Christ in the name of Jesus.

EXTRA RESOURCES FOR READING
Philippians 4:4-9., Romans 8:5-11., Romans 7:21-25

Giving Thanks for: --

I'm Praying for: --

Devotional Reflections On My Heart Today : ----------------------------------
----

Things I'm Still Struggling With : --

DAY 11
CONTROL YOUR TONGUE
James 3:1-12
MEMORY VERSE

Even so the tongue is a little member and boasts great things. See how great a forest a little fire kindles! James 3:5(Nkjv)

EXPOSITION

The very day you gave your life to Christ, you began that day a new life and journey towards perfection. Yes! You heard me right. Some would say, is it possible to be perfect in this sinful imperfect world? Yeah! If it's not possible to be perfect, the lord would not tell you in Mathew 5:48 that you "should therefore be perfect as our father in Heaven is perfect". The question is how then can you be perfect while leaving in this imperfect world?

In James 3: 2 the bible says "For we all stumble in many things. If anyone does not stumble in word, he is a perfect man, able also to bridle the whole body". This means that, if you can control your tongue and be master over your words, then you are gradually getting close to perfection. Jesus said in Mathew 15:11 that "Man is not defiled by what goes into their mouth but by what comes out of their mouth. Therefore brethren!! Guard your tongue!!!.

Many have destroyed their lives and destinies and sent helpers away by just some words which they spoke wrongly. A friend of mine used to say that it is better to keep your mouth shut if you have nothing to say than to open it and blow all dust. A fool sometimes look very wise when he's quiet than when he speaks and talks nonsense. Be wise.

PRAYERS FOR THE DAY

*Let the Power to bridle my tongue fall upon my life today in the name of Jesus.

*My tongue shall not send me to hell fire in Jesus name.

EXTRA RESOURCES FOR READING

Ecclesiastes 5:1-7., Proverbs 18: 20-21., Luke 6: 43-45.

Giving Thanks for: ---

I'm Praying for: --

Devotional Reflections On My Heart Today : ----------------------------------
----

Things I'm Still Struggling With : ---

DAY 12
PRAY UNTIL SOMETHING HAPPENS
Daniel 10:1-21
MEMORY VERSE

"Be anxious for nothing, but in everything by prayer and supplication, with thanksgiving, let your requests be made known to God" Philippians 4:6 (Nkjv)

EXPOSITION

If men would learn how to take their requests to God in prayers everyday instead of complaining to their fellow humans alone, life would be much easier to live, and things would happen much faster for them than it normally does. In the book of Luke 18:1 Jesus was speaking to his disciples saying that "Men ought always to pray and not to faint. Jesus was making us aware in this passage that most of the battles that we fight as Christians should be done first in the spiritual realm before we begin to see manifestations in the physical.

As a believer, you need to learn to discipline yourself when it comes to the place of prayers. If sleep would distract you while kneeling then stand on your feet and walk around your room praying. It is Christians who sleep, the devil is not sleeping. You have to persist in the place of prayers until something happens. The more you pray, the weaker the enemy becomes and after a while, the enemy gives up.

In the book of Daniel 10, we see how Daniel went before God in prayers and for 21 days he waited on his knees in fasting and praying until the answer came, because the prince of Persia did not allow the angel bringing the answers to the prayers to get through to Daniel. Beloved! You need to realize that those who kneel before God praying would stand in victory before any situation. Prayer works!

PRAYERS FOR THE DAY

*Oh lord empower me to pray without ceasing in Jesus name.

*You my prayer altar, receive the fresh fire of revival in the name of Jesus.

EXTRA RESOURCES FOR READING
1 Kings 17:1-24., 1 Kings 18:1-46., Ephesians 6:18-19.

Giving Thanks for:--

I'm Praying for:--

Devotional Reflections On My Heart Today :----------------------------
----

Things I'm Still Struggling With :--

DAY 13
CURSE CURSELESS SHALL NOT STAND
Galatians 3:13
MEMORY VERSE

"Christ has redeemed us from the curse of the law, having become a curse for us [for it is written, "Cursed is everyone who hangs on a tree]' Galatians 3:13 Nkjv

EXPOSITION

In the garden of Eden after the fall of man, God placed curses upon the man and the woman which chatted the course of their sojourn on this planet. The curse of hard labor and sweat on the man and the curse of Sorrow in childbearing on the woman. Unfortunately, man has labored under these curses since then and the devil also rejoices in this when man has no results to show for his hard work. That is an example of generational curse on man through our common ancestor Adam.

Apart from the curse of Eden on man, Curses can come on a man through no faults of his own, and when such curses are not broken, it follows man everywhere he goes. Jabez in 1 Chronicles:4 was an example by virtue of his birth. His mother placed the curse of sorrow on him through his name at birth. But Jabez cried out unto God and foundational curse of limitation that was upon his life was removed.

As a child of God, you do not have to labor under that curse of the law anymore. The moment you decide to give your life to Jesus, you automatically become a part of the family of Christ and his death on the cross redeems you from that curse of Eden placed upon the human race in the garden of Eden. The only thing left for you to do is to place a demand on heaven on your behalf and you'll be free to operate in dominion. Receive grace to call on God today in Jesus name.

PRAYERS FOR THE DAY

*By the power in the bloody Jesus, I am Redeemed from the cursed the law in the named Jesus.

*Generational curses in my life release me in the name of Jesus.

EXTRA RESOURCES FOR READING
Genesis 3:16-19., 1 Chronicles 4:9-10, Ezekiel 19:1-32

Giving Thanks for:---

I'm Praying for:--

Devotional Reflections On My Heart Today :------------------------------------
----

Things I'm Still Struggling With :---

DAY 14
LOVE SUFFERS LONG
1 Corinthians 13:1-8.
MEMORY VERSE
Love suffers long and is kind; love does not envy; love does not parade itself, is not puffed up".1 Corinthians 13:4. Nkjv

EXPOSITION

The first fruit of the spirit as outlined by Apostle Paul in the book of Galatians is love and in the book of 1 Corinthians 13:13 he referred to love as the greatest gift of the spirit saying "And now abide faith, hope, love, these three; but the greatest of these is love".

What does Apostle Paul mean by "love suffers long"? He simply means that love endures hardships, uncomfortable situations, doesn't give up easily on people, does not get angry easily especially when dealing with difficult people, it doesn't yell unnecessarily on the children or spouse when they err, would not start yelling profanities while in traffic if someone "cuts them off" but instead would rather say God bless you. It doesn't get tired of helping a fellow brother who always gets into trouble. Love gives and continues to give even when it seems not convenient without expecting anything in return.

Love doesn't just pack up and walk out of a church simply because a fellow believer offends him or her but would instead find a way to settle such a hurt with his brethren. If as a Christian you still cannot exercise all of the aforementioned things then God's kind of love is not yet in you. The Bible says if you obey every part of the law of God but do not have love then you are but like a sounding cymbal.

PRAYERS FOR THE DAY
*Oh God my father, release upon me the grace to love unconditionally in the name of Jesus.

*Every seed of hatred in me, die by the fire of God in Jesus name
EXTRA RESOURCES FOR READING
Galatians 5:1-End., Romans 13:1-10., Ephesians 3:16-17

Giving Thanks for:---

I'm Praying for:---

Devotional Reflections On My Heart Today :-----------------------------------
----

Things I'm Still Struggling With :---

------------------------------   ---

DAY 15
RISE UP AND WALK
Acts 3: 1 - 9.
MEMORY VERSE
Jesus saith unto him, Rise, take up thy bed and walk.
John 5:8 Kjv

EXPOSITION

In the book of Acts 3, Peter and John went into the temple at the 9th hour of prayers and a certain man who was blind from his mother's womb, always laying by the Gate called Beautiful looked at them begging for alms. Now there are two things that's worthy of note here. Firstly, the man was not named, but only described as a certain lame man which tells us that his problem has become the Name by which he is known and Secondly, laying at the gate that's Beautiful, whereas there's nothing beautiful in his personal life.

Does that situation sound familiar to you? Situations that kept this man down from birth has prevented him from manifesting his divine potentials and has now become his name. Peter fastened his eyes on him and said by implication that what you are expecting from me I cannot give unto you but what I'll give you is what your life needs to move you out of this limitation into your level of dominion and liberty.

I believe that must have come as a shock to the lame man because he must have been thinking that his condition is irreversible and so have accepted his fate, however, when the word of power and authority went out to him, every demonic barrier over his life was broken and he was never the same again. May the lord visit you today in the Name of Jesus.

PRAYERS FOR THE DAY
*Every arrow of limitation in my life die by fire in the name of Jesus.

*Whatever is keeping me from fulfilling my divine destiny on earth, release me today in the name of Jesus

EXTRA RESOURCES FOR READING
John 5:1-9., Mathew 9:1-8., Mark 2:1-12

Giving Thanks for:--

I'm Praying for:---

Devotional Reflections On My Heart Today :-------------------------------------
----

Things I'm Still Struggling With :---

DAY 16
ALWAYS ON TIME
John 11: 1 - 45
MEMORY VERSE

"Jesus said unto her, I am the resurrection, and the life: he that believeth in me, though he were dead, yet shall he live". John 11:25..KJV)

EXPOSITION

In this passage above the Bible tells us about Lazarus, the brother of Mary; the lady who anointed the feet of Jesus with oil and wiped it off with her hair. This Lazarus was a friend of Jesus who he loved so much. Lazarus was sick unto death and Mary sent to Jesus and told him that Lazarus whom you love is sick, but Jesus did not respond or follow them immediately because it was not yet time.

Now talk about connection, Lazarus has it, because he is a personal friend of Jesus along with his sisters Martha and Mary. So, at this point, Jesus hearing their voices was not the issue, but it wasn't yet time. Sometimes, we pray very hard, fast for long periods of time, deny ourselves of certain comforts just because we want God to do a particular thing for us, but God still seems to be telling us that it's not yet time.

We come to church, attend every meeting, throw ourselves into God's service and try our best to do everything right, both spiritually and physically, but still it seems God is not listening. Then we feel abandoned as if God has disappointed us just like Mary and Martha must have felt initially in this instance. I have good news for you today, "God is never late to any situation" because when he shows up, things turn around! He makes all things beautiful in his time.

PRAYERS FOR THE DAY

*Oh God of time and Season, appear by fire in my situation in the name of Jesus.

*I shall not miss my God's perfect timing for my life in Jesus name

EXTRA RESOURCES FOR READING
Habakkuk 2:1-End., Acts 9:36-43., John 7:1-9.

Giving Thanks for:---

I'm Praying for:---

Devotional Reflections On My Heart Today :--

Things I'm Still Struggling With :---

-----------------   --
--- --

DAY 17
WHEN ONE DOOR CLOSES
1 Peter 5:1-11
MEMORY VERSE

But the God of all grace, who hath called us unto his eternal glory by Christ Jesus, after that ye have suffered a while, make you perfect, stablish, strengthen, settle you.1 Peter 5:10 Kjv

EXPOSITION

In the journey of life, people often meet with situations and circumstances that sometimes make them to wonder why things are just not working or going the way they desire or dream about. Well, I got news for you "Life is full of ups and downs, roadblocks and stumbling blocks, mountains and valleys" especially if you are a true believer who desires to move forward in life.

As a believer, when things don't go your way, that is not the time to complain and murmur, but time for you to glorify God and believe that God is turning things around in your Favor. Maybe everyone around has turned against you, remember Job in the scriptures, after he lost everything he has ever worked for, all in just one single day. Even his friends and wives turned against him, yet he did not sin and his attitude and disposition towards God during that difficult moments made him to pass that test of faith.

God restored everything he lost during that trial period back to him in multiple folds. In 1 Peter 5:10 the bible says, "After you have suffered a little while, the lord is able to establish, strength and settle you". Whatever the situation is, the lord is able to turn it around for his glory meaning that meaning when one door closes another door opens.

PRAYERS FOR THE DAY

*Oh God arise and change my story for your glory Jesus name

*Every power standing at my door of greatness to stop me, release me by fire in the name of Jesus.

EXTRA RESOURCES FOR READING
Acts 16: 16-40., Romans 18:18-28., Job 42:1-13

Giving Thanks for:--

I'm Praying for:---

Devotional Reflections On My Heart Today :------------------------------------

----

Things I'm Still Struggling With :---

------------------------ --

-- --

DAY 18
RENEW YOUR MIND
Romans 12:1-14
MEMORY VERSE

And be not conformed to this world: but be ye transformed by the renewing of your mind, that ye may prove what is that good, and acceptable, and perfect, will of God. Romans 12:2 Kjv

EXPOSITION

What does it mean to "Renew your mind"? To renew a thing means to refresh, to make new, throw away the old nature and taking up a new look, character or attributes. Your Mind in the biblical sense refers to your inner man, the real you, the very center of your being i.e. the one that controls all that is called you. Scientifically, that can be referred to as your Mental Faculty or Spiritually speaking called your Spirit man which symbolizes who you really are.

So, putting the two together, to renew the mind means to transform your inner or spirit man into something that is fresh and without blemish. This is exactly what happens at the time of the new birth when a new peace, joy and tranquility that you and only you can fathom came over your life and that's being born anew or born again. However, a lot of Christians in this age claim to be born again but the spirit inside them is not renewed.

A lot of things that are not even supposed to be mentioned among unbelievers have now crept into the lives and body of Christ today simply because the mind is not renewed, and they have slipped back into the world. Now it has become difficult to differentiate between Christians and unbelievers. The question for you as you meditate on these words is this "Are you renewed in your mind"?

PRAYERS FOR THE DAY

*My father, My Father, if I have been damaged spiritually, oh lord repair me in the name of Jesus.

*Oh Lord, break me down and remold me again in Jesus Name.

EXTRA RESOURCES FOR READING

Philippians 4:4-9., 2 Timothy 1:6-10., 2 Corinthians 5:1-17

Giving Thanks for:---

I'm Praying for:--

Devotional Reflections On My Heart Today :------------------------------------
----

Things I'm Still Struggling With :--

-------------------------   ---

DAY 19
IS JESUS YOUR EVERYTHING?
Galatians 5:16 – 26
MEMORY VERSE
I say then: Walk in the Spirit, and you shall not fulfill the lust of the flesh. Galatians 5:16 Kjv

EXPOSITION
In verse 17 of our text for today, the bible says, "for the flesh lusts against the spirit and the spirit against the flesh, and these are contrary to one another so that you do not do the things that you wish". We see in this passage that in life there are two opposing forces, one for good and the other of evil. These two forces are constantly crying for attention in the day to day life of humans since creation.

The Bible even acknowledges it there, that you do not do the things that you wish but instead do those things you really do not want to do. Is it not surprising to see that in Romans 7:15, Apostle Paul also said "For what I am doing I do not understand, for what I will do, that I do not practice, but what I hate that I do."

If Jesus is your everything, even though these opposing forces are kicking in everyday as it was for Apostle Paul, as a child of God who is walking on a Christian race to heaven, you will not yield to these attempts by the enemy to bring you down. Even if you fall or the enemy knocks you down, you would not stay knocked down, but you'll quickly rise and run back to God in true repentance. May you receive grace and boldness to properly align yourself with the lord in Jesus Name.

PRAYERS FOR THE DAY
*Oh God my father, create in me a clean heart and renew a right spirit within me in the name of Jesus.

*Lord help me to make you my all in all every day in Jesus name.

EXTRA RESOURCES FOR READING
Daniel 3:1-18., Job 13:1-16., Romans 12:1-5

Giving Thanks for:---

I'm Praying for:---

Devotional Reflections On My Heart Today :---

Things I'm Still Struggling With :--

----------------------   ---
--- --

DAY 20
LORD OPEN MY EYES
Ecclesiastes 9:10-18
MEMORY VERSE
Open thou mine eyes, that I may behold wondrous things out of thy law. Psalms 19:18 Kjv

EXPOSITION

As Christians who cry daily to the lord for help and deliverance, God wants to reveal things to us but simply because the enemy has put a veil upon people's vision, it becomes difficult to receive any information from the lord even when he speaks because where there is darkness there can never be revelation except God shines his light.

In Proverbs 28:18, the Bible says, "where there is no vision the people perish". And if there is no vision, there can never be revelation and where there is no revelation there cannot be knowledge because revelation brings revolution. It takes divine revelation for someone to discover his true potentials, it takes divine revelation for someone to know that he or she is operating below his/her divinely ordained standard and ability.

When you catch the revelation of who God has ordained you to be, it stirs up something inside of you and that yields a revolution. The very moment revolution starts, the divinely ordained potentials and abilities inside of you begin to manifest and you automatically no longer the same person, then life, circumstances and situations begin to turn around. Where there is knowledge, there is liberty. May the lord open your spiritual and physical eyes as you read this in Jesus Name.

PRAYERS FOR THE DAY

*Oh God my father, open thou my eyes to see deep and secret things that would transform my life in the name of Jesus.

*Lord I want to see you, open my eyes in the name of Jesus.

EXTRA RESOURCES FOR READING
Mark 10:46-52., Genesis 21:8-21., 2 Kings 6: 15-20

Giving Thanks for:--

I'm Praying for:---

Devotional Reflections On My Heart Today :--

Things I'm Still Struggling With :---

------------------------- ---

--- --

PRAYER OF AGREEMENT
Mathew 18:18-20
MEMORY VERSE

"Again, I say unto you, that if two of you shall agree on earth as touching anything that they shall ask, it shall be done for them of my Father which is in heaven" Mathew 18:19 Nkjv

EXPOSITION

Sometime ago, I watched a wildlife documentary in which two Massai tribal men of east Africa put a pride of lions to flight and taking away a large chunk of the lions kill by simply kneeling down and rising up together at once and walking together straight towards the lions armed with not more than a butcher knife and a stick. The lions all fled abandoning their kill in fear, giving the two Massai men enough time to quickly make a spoil of the lion's meal. That's the power of agreement. When we walk in agreement, we get things done more effortlessly than when done single handedly.

In James 5:16, it is written "Confess your faults one to another, and pray one for another, that ye may be healed. The effectual fervent prayer of a righteous man availeth much." Christians nowadays are very secretive, always wanting to keep their personal problems to themselves. This is very understandable because there are so many busy bodies in the fold, so it's wise to tread cautiously.

However, many battles would be won for believers if they would just put off pride and humbly find fellow believers who they can join their faith with by Tapping into this irresistible force of agreement in oneness of spirit to put the enemy to flight.

PRAYERS FOR THE DAY

*By the power in the blood of Jesus, the devil shall not get me through isolation from other believers in Jesus name.

*Power to decree and come to pass fall upon me in Jesus name.

EXTRA RESOURCES FOR READING

Ecclesiastes 4:1-12., Leviticus 26:8., Deuteronomy 32:27-31

Giving Thanks for:--

I'm Praying for:--

Devotional Reflections On My Heart Today :--

Things I'm Still Struggling With :---

--------------------------   --

-- --

DAY 22
BROKENNESS
Psalms 34:1-18
MEMORY VERSE

"The LORD is nigh unto them that are of a broken heart;
and saveth such as be of a contrite spirit" Psalms 34:18 Kjv

EXPOSITION

Have you ever seen a broken horse before? Yeah! I bet you have!!. Let me quickly explain what a broken horse is. When any horse is going to be ridden on for the first time, the horse makes every attempt to throw off the rider and it's not always a pleasant experience for both the rider and the horse. However, if the rider can hang onto the horseback long enough and doesn't fall off, then the horse succumbs to the new authority, inadvertently admitting that the rider is boss and from then forward, such a horse can be ridden anytime by anyone.

That's called a broken horse, because at that point it doesn't have its own free will anymore, but only operates based solely on the will of the master. Now to the Christian life. An unbroken Christian is one who has not yet submitted completely to the will of the lord, but instead is still controlled by his/her passions, hence cannot be used of the master. Such a person is still completely ruled and directed by the dictates of the flesh and untamed, thus cannot be used of the master.

Such Passions like every works of the flesh mentioned in Galatians 5:19-21 cannot be found in the life of a broken Christian." A broken Christian is completely dead to self and remains so every day like Apostle Paul said in 1 Corinthians 15:31(Nkjv) "I die daily". Cry unto the lord, tell him to break you down, to be fit for use in his service.

PRAYERS FOR THE DAY

*Oh lord, please drag me into the Porter's house this day and break me down and remold me again in the name of Jesus.

*Lord make me a vessel unto honor in your vineyard in Jesus name.

EXTRA RESOURCES FOR READING
Galatians 5:1-End., Psalms 51: 1- 19., Jeremiah 18:1-6

Giving Thanks for:--

I'm Praying for:--

Devotional Reflections On My Heart Today :------------------------------------
----

Things I'm Still Struggling With :--

DAY 23
COME OUT OF THE VALLEY
Psalms 143: 1-End.
MEMORY VERSE

Cause me to hear thy lovingkindness in the morning; for in thee do I trust: cause me to know the way wherein I should walk; for I lift up my soul unto thee. Psalms 143:8 Kjv.

EXPOSITION

What does it mean to be in the valley? Geography defines a valley as a low land between two hills/mountains. Some people decide to live permanently on the valley while some make up their minds they want to be on the mountain top. Figuratively speaking, valley life is lifestyle below perfect, but irrespective of where you find yourself you don't have to be contented with that level because there is always a much better level you can get to or attain.

You need to know that, it is not the lords perfect will for anyone of his children to dwell perpetually in the valley because the mountain top experience is there to enjoy however, you cannot enjoy that abundant mountain top life if your settle for whatever life throws your way. Therefore, refuse to settle for less than the perfect of life because there's still much space left for you at the top to occupy.

Whoever stays in the valley will experience various forms of insults, tragedies and neglect, because whatever garbage gets washed off the mountain, finds its way down the valley and whoever is in there takes in all rubbish. You can change your world by speaking unto that valley situation. Beloved! Get out of the valley and find your way to the top. The lord wants you up there! Go for it!!

PRAYERS FOR THE DAY

*Every evil plantation in my life keeping me perpetually in the valley, I curse your root, wither and die in Jesus name.

*I break out of the valley, unto the mountaintop in Jesus name.

EXTRA RESOURCES FOR READING
Ezekiel 37:1-End.,1 Samuel 2:1-10., Psalm 23:1-End

Giving Thanks for:---

I'm Praying for:--

Devotional Reflections On My Heart Today :-----------------------------------
----

Things I'm Still Struggling With :--

-------------------------   ---
-- --

DAY 24
YOU ARE NOT HELPLESS
Isaiah 41:10-13.

MEMORY VERSE
Fear thou not; for I am with thee, be not dismayed; for I am thy God: I will strengthen thee; yea, I will help thee; yea, I will uphold thee with the right hand of my righteousness. Isaiah 41:10 Kjv

EXPOSITION!
Beloved, it perfect normal that sometimes, people feel helpless and it seems as if there is no way ahead. Maybe sometimes you also feel as if life is battering you and it seems as if you are on the receiving end of the negative side of life. Maybe helpers are so far away from you and you don't even have anywhere or any other person to turn to.

In the book of Psalms 123 verses 1-2, the Bible says I will lift up mine eyes unto the hills, from whence cometh my help. My help cometh from the Lord, which made heaven and earth. He would not suffer your feet to be moved". The lord is telling you in this passage that help is just close by, if only you can just call on him. In Mathew 7:7, he says Ask and you shall receive, seek and you shall find, Knock and the door shall be open, then beloved, what's stopping you from asking as much as you want? He has given you a blank check.

The lord is very much interested in making sure that all his children are enjoying the very best of life. However, God would not force anything down your throat because he has given man the power of choice. So, if you need help, all you need is to call out for help directly up into the heavenlies. Don't just sit down and complain about the situation, talk to the lord about it and help would be sent your way.

PRAYERS FOR THE DAY
*Divine help from the throne of grace, locate me today in the name of Jesus.

*My faith looks up to you oh lord, send me help in Jesus name.

EXTRA RESOURCES FOR READING
Psalms 123: 1-End., Mathew 7: 1-8., 1 Kings 17:7-16

Giving Thanks for:---

I'm Praying for:---

Devotional Reflections On My Heart Today :-----------------------------------
----

Things I'm Still Struggling With :---

DAY 25
HE WANTS YOU TO ASK
Mathew 7:7-12
MEMORY VERSE
"Ask, and it will be given to you; seek, and you will find; knock, and it will be opened to you. For everyone who asks receives, and he who seeks finds, and to him who knocks it will be opened. Mathew 7:7-8 Nkjv

EXPOSITION
God is our father and he has told us through his word that "he is the one that has the cattle on a thousand hills" (Psalm 50:10) he says the Silver and the Gold is his and he gives it to whosoever asks. Therefore, if your father "God" has all the worlds possessions in his hands then why would you his child begin to suffer?

The answer is that many children of God don't even know their rights, neither do they know that the resources of heaven and earth is at their disposal anytime they so need it if only they know how to ask.

Many are sick in their mortal bodies and need spare parts to replace the faulty one. Little do they know that help is just a prayer point away. All they need is to tap into the storeroom of heaven to pick up a spare part for themselves and the problem would be over.

Whatever the problem is, please take it to God in prayers just like Daniel did, and you'll be surprised how quickly help would show up for you, instead of complaining or trying to figure it out on your own because it is written in the book of 1 Samuel 2:9b that "By strength shall no man prevail". Don't just resign to fate, Don't give up! Get down on your knees and pray. Help is on the way!

PRAYERS FOR THE DAY
*Oh God that makes a way where there is no way, make a way for me in the name of Jesus.

*Divine abundance that would announce the greatness of my God, locate me today in the name of Jesus.

EXTRA RESOURCES FOR READING
Haggai 2:6-9., 3 JOHN 2-3., Psalms 50:1-11

Giving Thanks for:---

I'm Praying for:--

Devotional Reflections On My Heart Today :--

Things I'm Still Struggling With :--

-------------------   ---

--- --

DAY 26
OPPRESSION SHALL BE FAR FROM YOU
Isaiah 54: 1 - 15.

MEMORY VERSE

In righteousness shalt thou be established: thou shalt be far from oppression; for thou shalt not fear: and from terror; for it shall not come near thee. Isaiah 54:14 Kjv.

EXPOSITION

One of the weapons the Devil uses to deal terribly with people in the world today is the weapon of oppression. Looking at our world today we see various forms of oppression in the lives of people either physically or spiritually. Some have been plagued with oppression right from the womb even before they were born as in the case of the man who was born blind in the book of John 9:1-7 or the one who has been lame from birth in Acts 3:1 -13 sitting at the beautiful gate.

Some suffer oppressions even in their dreams in which case the demons come to either press them down while sleeping or they are constantly pursued in their dreams. They run and run and run till they wake up in the morning tired and exhausted. For some, it is hallucination of various types, some hear voices and it's just as if they should just die and end it all.

The night sleep that is supposed to be a peaceful thing to make them refreshed when they wake up turns to nightmares. Some are even afraid to go to bed each night because of what they would likely encounter in their sleep. Some are under financial oppression, seemingly impossible to make ends meet and constantly in debt. All these are works of the enemy. If you are under any of these situations, the lord is available to deliver you if only you can just trust in him.

PRAYERS FOR THE DAY

*Oppressions of the night targeting my life, release me and die, in the Name of Jesus!

*Arrows of oppression depart from my life in the name of Jesus.

EXTRA RESOURCES FOR READING
Luke 13:10-17., Ecclesiastes 7:1-8.,

Giving Thanks for:--

I'm Praying for:---

Devotional Reflections On My Heart Today :----------------------------------
----

Things I'm Still Struggling With :--

------------------- ---

AFFLICTION SHALL NOT RISE THE SECOND TIME
Nahum1:7-11
MEMORY VERSE
What do you conspire against the Lord? He will make an utter end of it. Affliction will not rise up a second time. Nahum 1:9 Nkjv

EXPOSITION
We sometimes see people who are so oppressed mentally that they cannot think straight again. They suffer memory losses that important details that should move their lives forward or that should get them out of trouble are forgotten only to be remembered after the evil occur. That's why in the book of Ecclesiastes 7:7a, the Bible says, "Surely oppression makes the wise Mad".

It is oppression that makes a supposedly learned person who desires to be rich to go seek for financial advice from someone who is obviously broke and needs help himself. However, the promise of the lord in Isaiah 54:14 is that you shall be far from oppression. In Luke 13:10-17, we see a woman who the enemy has kept under oppression, bent over for 18 years. But the day she encountered the lord, the oppression left her.

The Bible says the Devil came only but to kill and to steal and destroy but Jesus has come to give eternal life. If you'll call upon the lord today, oppression would depart from your life because, one thing is certain here, when an oppressed comes in contact with the master the oppression has no choice but to leave. Receive deliverance from every satanic oppression in your life today in the name of Jesus.

PRAYERS FOR THE DAY
*Arrows of affliction operating in my life, come out and die in the name of Jesus!

*Oh lord arise and purge every territory in my life that the enemy has occupied in the name of Jesus.

EXTRA RESOURCES FOR READING
Acts 3:1-13., John 9: 1-7

Giving Thanks for:--

I'm Praying for:--

Devotional Reflections On My Heart Today :----------------------------------
----

Things I'm Still Struggling With :--

--------------------------   --

DAY 28
HELPERS OF DESTINY
Esther 2: 1 -20.
MEMORY VERSE
"For it is God who is at work in you, both to will and to work for His good Pleasure". Philippians 2:13 Nkjv

EXPOSITION

God has not created anyone who is supposed to be a self-sufficient island. I mean someone who has everything and doesn't need anything or any help from anyone. Even the super-rich and stupendously wealthy on earth still requires some sort of help or assistance from someone at one time or the other such that if such help or connections do not come at the right time, life changing opportunities might be lost forever.

In the scriptures we come across several examples of divinely ordained destiny helpers, who appeared suddenly on behalf of people. In the book of Esther, after the parents of Esther died, Mordecai adopted her as his own child and when it was time for a new queen to be chosen in the land of Babylon, Modecai packaged Esther very well and coached her on what to say and how to comport herself in the presence of the king.

Though Esther was the least qualified in the land being a common slave girl, her helper propelled her to her place of Destiny. What of David who had a divine helper in "Jonathan" the son of his arch enemy King Saul. That helper pushed him forward till he achieved his divine position. At some points in life, we all need someone like that around us. I pray that you find people to push you into fulfilling your divine destiny in life in Jesus Name.

PRAYERS FOR THE DAY

*Wherever my divine helpers are located, oh God arise and connect me with them in the name of Jesus!

*Oh lord repackage me for greatness in the name of Jesus.

EXTRA RESOURCES FOR READING
Genesis 18:1-End., Genesis 40:6-7., 2 kings 5:1-End

Giving Thanks for:--

I'm Praying for:--

Devotional Reflections On My Heart Today :-----------------------------------
----

Things I'm Still Struggling With :---

-----------------------   --

DAY 29
GOD CAN USE YOUR ENEMY TO HELP YOU
Psalms 121:1-End
MEMORY VERSE
I will lift up my eyes to the hills, From whence comes my help? My help comes from the Lord, Who made heaven and earth. Psalms 121:1-2 Nkjv
EXPOSITION
Pharaoh was the arch enemy of the Israelites, But in Exodus 2:1-10, Pharaoh's daughter was the one used by God to save the baby Moses at birth while Pharaoh was busy executing all other male Hebrew children born at that time. The same household who decreed the death of all the male Hebrew children eventually supervised the upbringing of Moses in the palace.

God can turn your sworn enemy to your destiny helpers who would connect you to the top. They would bear your burdens as if it is their own. They would be strategically positioned to help you navigate through barriers and obstacles. Even when it's not convenient for them they stick their necks out, to bail you out of unfavorable circumstances. When God is involved, they would spend their hard-earned resources on you and would not expect anything in return.

They are there to push you forward when opportunities appear and would not stop until they see you succeed. Such helpers would be the voice that speaks on your behalf, when you are not there to speak for yourself. At one point or the other we all need them in our lives in order to move forward. I pray for you as you read that the lord would connect you supernaturally to your divine helpers of destiny in the course of your existence on earth in the name of Jesus.

PRAYERS FOR THE DAY
*Whether the enemy likes it or not, I receive divine help today in the Name of Jesus

*Uncommon help from above, locate me in the name of Jesus.
EXTRA RESOURCES FOR READING
1 Kings 17:12-End., Psalms 121:1- End., Exodus 2:1-10

Giving Thanks for:---

I'm Praying for:---

Devotional Reflections On My Heart Today :-----------------------------------
----

Things I'm Still Struggling With :---

HE WILL STRENGTHEN YOU
2 Corinthians 12:8-10.
MEMORY VERSE
"And He said to me, "My grace is sufficient for you, for My strength is made perfect in weakness." Therefore, most gladly I will rather boast in my infirmities, that the power of Christ may rest upon me". II Corinthians 12:9 Nkjv
EXPOSITION
In the book of Isaiah 41:10, the Bible says "So do not fear, for I am with you; do not be dismayed, for I am your God. I will strengthen you and help you; I will uphold you with my righteous right hand. The lord is saying if you are weak in your mortal body, maybe you are currently sick, hospitalized, maybe emotionally you are currently discouraged and helpless, Maybe you feel currently that you don't even have the strength to go on and you are at the verge of caving in and giving up.

The lord is saying this morning that he will strengthen you because his strength is made perfect in your weakness. Psalm 46:1-3 says "God is our refuge and strength, an ever-present help in trouble". This means that no matter your level of weakness at this time, the lord is ever present to help if only you're willing to call upon him.

He said come unto me all you who labor and are heavy laden and I will give you rest for my yoke is easy and my burden is light. The lord is ever there to go with you every step of the way. Though it may seem he is not there, but he is the ever-silent companion always there in times of trouble. Help is on the way.
PRAYERS FOR THE DAY
*Oh God my father, my help in time of trouble, arise and fight my battles in the name of Jesus.

*Lord I need your strength everyday of my life in Jesus Name.
EXTRA RESOURCES FOR READING
Colossians 1: 11-20., Psalms 9:9-10

Giving Thanks for:--

I'm Praying for:--

Devotional Reflections On My Heart Today :-------------------------------------
----

Things I'm Still Struggling With :---

HOLD UNTO HIS PROMISES
Deuteronomy 31:3-8
MEMORY VERSE
Be strong and of good courage, do not fear nor be afraid of them; for the LORD your God, He *is* the One who goes with you. He will not leave you nor forsake you." Deuteronomy 31:8 Nkjv

EXPOSITION
There was this story of a man who had a dream seeing himself walking with Jesus on a very lonely road and all of a sudden, some terrible storms arise and he no longer saw Jesus but instead saw only a pair of feet walking which he assumed were his own. However, when the storms cease, the other pair of feet appears.

This man was confused and angry at Jesus, so he challenged Jesus saying, why do you always abandon me and vanish when every time the storm starts raging because I only see my set of footprints in the sand as I go along. Then Jesus smiled and said to him, those foot prints you saw were not yours but they are mine because during those trouble times, I was carrying you on my wings and that was the reason why you were able to go through those moments successfully.

Beloved! Sometimes it might seem God abandoned you especially during trouble times when you have cried for help, but he seems so far away. Know for a fact, he's always there, watching over you every step of the way. He would strengthen you no matter what the situation is. He's carrying you on the eagle's wings just like he did for the Israelites when they went through the Red Sea carrying them on the eagle's wings in Exodus 19:4. Keep trusting! He'll not fail you.

PRAYERS FOR THE DAY
*The strength of God to continue this Christian journey and not grow weary, lord release unto me now in the Name of Jesus!

*I shall not be a failure in my daily walk with God in Jesus name.

EXTRA RESOURCES FOR READING
Isaiah 26:1-4., Isaiah 43:1-3., Psalms 145:18 - 19

Giving Thanks for:--

I'm Praying for:--

Devotional Reflections On My Heart Today :------------------------------------
----

Things I'm Still Struggling With :--

DAY 32
THINK ON THESE THINGS
Philippians 4: 6 - 9.
MEMORY VERSE
"Finally, brethren, whatsoever things are true, whatsoever things are honest, whatsoever things are just, whatsoever things are pure, whatsoever things are lovely, whatsoever things are of good report; if there be any virtue, and if there be any praise, think on these things. Philippians 4:8KJV.

EXPOSITION
An old Proverb says, "A man is what he thinks all day". Beloved, our lives are controlled and shaped by our thoughts and this is why Apostle Paul is saying in the verse above that we should think only on those honorable things.

Whatever a man would do has already occurred at the thought level before transforming into actions. The Bible told us to guard our hearts and minds diligently because out of it flows the issues of life (Proverbs 4:23). Whatsoever is stored up inside your heart is what your words and actions begin to be shaped by.

The word of God tells us that, it is not what goes inside that makes one unclean but what comes out. For it is from inside the heart that various forms of evil thoughts idolatry, fornication, adultery etc. comes out and all these defiles a man. The lord wants us as his children to channel out thought process only towards those things which edifies, and which allows the spirit of God to dwell inside us peaceably. May you receive a clearer spirit filled thought process in Jesus Name.

PRAYERS FOR THE DAY
*Create in me a clean heart and renew a right spirit within me in the name of Jesus!

* Power to guard my mind with all diligence fall upon me in the name of Jesus

EXTRA RESOURCES FOR READING
Philipians4:1-8., Proverbs 24:1-4

Giving Thanks for:--

I'm Praying for:--

Devotional Reflections On My Heart Today :---------------------------------
----

Things I'm Still Struggling With :---

DAY 33
THE BATTLE OVER THE MIND
Romans 7:17-23 Nkjv
MEMORY VERSE
But I see another law in my members, warring against the law of my mind, and bringing me into captivity to the law of sin which is in my members Romans 7:23

EXPOSITION
There is a battle over the control of the mind of man between two opposing forces i.e. the good vs the bad. As a child of God, this is a battle that you must strive and ensure that the battle is not won by the Bad forces. Therefore, you must make a conscious effort to skew your mind towards those things which are good always.

The book of Luke 6:45 says "A good man out of the good treasure of his heart bringeth forth that which is good; and an evil man out of the evil treasure of his heart bringeth forth that which is evil: for out of the abundance of the heart the mouth speaks". The lord wants us as his children to channel our thought process only to think about those things which edifies, and which allows the spirit of God to dwell inside us peaceably. The bible says we should guard our hearts diligently, for out of it springs the issues of life. (Proverbs 4:23)

You must constantly ask the Holy Spirit to help you renew your mind everyday so you may be fully in tune with him. Remember, your thoughts breeds actions, actions breeds character and character breeds destiny. You need to cry to God to renew a right spirit within you daily. This you can do by dwelling on the word of God and asking the Holy Spirit to empower you to continually guard your mind. Know this! Your mind is like the Computer! Garbage in! Garbage out!.

PRAYERS FOR THE DAY
*Oh lord empower me not to harbor any thought that would grieve your spirit in the Name of Jesus

*Every battle raging in my mind release me in Jesus name.

EXTRA RESOURCES FOR READING
Psalms 51:10-19., Mathew 15:16-20

Giving Thanks for:---

I'm Praying for:--

Devotional Reflections On My Heart Today :---

Things I'm Still Struggling With :---

----------------------------   --

DAY 34
POWER OF ASSOCIATION
1 Corinthians 15:33-34.
MEMORY VERSE
"Be not deceived: evil communications corrupt good manners"1 Corinthians 15:33. Nkjv

EXPOSITION

An old Proverb says, "Show me your friends and I'll show you who you are". Beloved! That's the power of association. It's just natural for people to begin to behave, act and reason like those they interact with the most. That's why it's very important as believers to be careful who we keep in our inner circle of friends if truly we are serious about making it to heaven as our final home.

The bible says in 2 Corinthians 6:14 "Do not be unequally yoked together with an unbeliever or what fellowship has light got to do with darkness". When as a child of the kingdom all your best friends are chronic unbelievers, it most likely those friends are the ones who would likely draw you away from the way of the cross unto compromising your salvation.

It's just like you the believer is the person standing on a pedestal while your unbelieving associations are the ones on the ground. If you both hold hands and walk together, I think it's very obvious that the person walking on the lower ground can easily pull you that's on the elevated pedestal down to his level. Now I believe you understand clearly the impact that your associations can have on your journey in life. Your associations on earth can determine your place in eternity if you aren't careful! Be wise!

PRAYERS FOR THE DAY

*Power to detach myself from every unprofitable associations fall upon my life in the name of Jesus.

*Lord give me power to break off from every evil association within the circle of my life in the name of Jesus.

EXTRA RESOURCES FOR READING
2 Corinthians 6:14-17., Proverbs 9:1-10

Giving Thanks for:---

I'm Praying for:---

Devotional Reflections On My Heart Today :-------------------------------------
----

Things I'm Still Struggling With :---

---------------------------- --

WALK WITH THE WISE
Proverbs 13:18-25
MEMORY VERSE
He who walks with wise men will be wise, But the companion of fools will be destroyed. Proverbs 13:20 Nkjv

EXPOSITION

This passage above makes it clear that when you desire more wisdom, then you need to find people who are more learned, more experienced and better equipped than you to associate with or add to your circle. That way you can learn from them and by so doing you'll begin to accumulate more knowledge and wisdom for progress.

The book of Proverbs 27:17 says, "As Iron sharpens Iron, So, one person sharpens another". When you keep wise and intelligent people as your friends, it begins to rub off on you after a while because you tap from their wealth of wisdom and people begin to see you as wise too. Rich people only flock around the rich because like begets like and by so doing they tend to get richer because through such associations they make new business connections that bring in more wealth unto them.

As Parents also, children tend to pattern their behaviors and characters after those of their parents because those are the people they spend most times around and it's just natural to pick after them. This means as parents we need to build a Godly character so that we might be able to raise Godly children. My prayer for you today is that you would be bold enough to make the right changes to your circle of friends in the name of Jesus.

PRAYERS FOR THE DAY

*I receive power to detach myself from every negative influence around my life in the name of Jesus.

* Every satanic magnet attracting unprofitable friends towards me, be roasted by fire in the name of Jesus.

EXTRA RESOURCES FOR READING
Psalms 26:1-5., 2 Timothy 4:9-18

Giving Thanks for:--

I'm Praying for:--

Devotional Reflections On My Heart Today :------------------------------------
----

Things I'm Still Struggling With :--

-------------------- --

DAY 36
THE GOLDEN RULE
Mathew7:11-13
MEMORY VERSE
"And as ye would that men should do to you, do ye also to them likewise". Luke 6:31 Kjv.
EXPOSITION
There is a rule in the scriptures called the "Golden Rule" that by implication says whatever goes around comes around. This is found in the Sermon on the Mount given by our lord Jesus Christ in Mathew 7:12 saying "we should do exactly unto others what we would want them do unto u". The lord is saying here that if you are not able to accept certain kinds of treatment from another person, then morality bestows it upon you to make sure you do not give the same treatment to someone else. Funny enough, people often want to be treated better than they treat others while completely forgetting the golden rule.

The bible says "with the same measure by which you measure out to someone else, by that same measure would it be measured back unto you (Luke 6:38b., Mathew 7:2b). Why would you as a person offer protection and covering for your own children, while you subject other people's children to emotional torture and avoidable abuse.

In your place of work, why would you join forces with others to gang up against another person till they are fired when all the conspiracy is only based on envy and jealousy. Or why would you be angry for no just cause with a fellow human simply because he/she is progressing and you are not and as a result, you try to bring that person down from their post of success. Remember, God is a righteous judge and he is watching.

PRAYERS FOR THE DAY
*Oh lord my father, empower me to make the lord Jesus my focus every day in the name of Jesus.

* Power to die to self, fall upon my life in the name of Jesus.
EXTRA RESOURCES FOR READING
Mathew 7:1-End., Luke 6:1-End

Giving Thanks for:---

I'm Praying for:--

Devotional Reflections On My Heart Today :----------------------------------
----

Things I'm Still Struggling With :--

--------------------   --

DAY 37
BE ANGRY BUT SIN NOT
Ephesians 4:25-32
MEMORY VERSE
"Be angry, and do not sin": do not let the sun go down on your wrath, nor give place to the devil. Ephesians 4:26-27 Nkjv

EXPOSITION

Anger is an emotion, and the lord God put them there for a purpose. Jesus himself was angry at certain point during his ministry which was expressed in John 2:13-17. That was a holy anger but the danger in this for Christians is for you to get angry unjustly to the point of falling into sin. As hard as it may seem to do, it is definitely possible to do and that's why the lord told us in that verse above not to sin whenever we are angry, because if he can do it, then we can do it too.

Jesus said in Mathew 5:22a that "That whosoever is angry with his brother without a cause shall be in danger of the judgment" and there's a proverb that says "whoever must destroy another in other to achieve success would also have destruction awaiting him as sentinel at the post of his/her success. Just in case your anger is because of the success of your fellow man.

When you are angry over someone else's success, then you are wishing something bad should happen to that person because you believe you are more deserving of that success than that other person. That is called envy with bitterness and there's nothing Godly in that. Jesus is our example and let every character and action be patterned towards Christ's kind of life. May you receive grace to live an anger free life in Jesus Name.

PRAYERS FOR THE DAY

*Oh lord my father, give me grace to deal with and subdue every seed of anger and bitterness in me in Jesus Name.

*You spirit of anger in me, get out of my life in Jesus name.

EXTRA RESOURCES FOR READING
Galatians 6:7-15., Genesis 8:18-22., Proverbs 14:29-30

Giving Thanks for:--

I'm Praying for:--

Devotional Reflections On My Heart Today :----------------------------------
----

Things I'm Still Struggling With :--

--------------------   --   --

DAY 38
RESPECT IS RECIPROCAL
Romans 13:1-8
MEMORY VERSE

Pay to all what is owed to them: taxes to whom taxes are owed, revenue to whom revenue is owed, respect to whom respect is owed, honor to whom honor is owed. Romans 13:7 Cev

EXPOSITION

Naturally, People want respect, appreciation and affection whether they deserve it or not. Jesus understood this nature in man and used it to promote godly behavior in that sermon on the mount. The question is this, Do you want to be shown respect? Then respect others. Do you crave a kind word? Then speak words of kindness to others. You have to realize that like begets like and the natural law of karma automatically returns to you, what you do unto others in due course.

The memory verse above tells us that we should show respect to whom respect is due. As a human being, you know when someone deserves respect and when they do not deserve it, because the power to know good from evil resides inside man and that's why God is not forcing you as a man to do it, but gives you the option to choose what to do. If you owe money, pay up because one day, it'll be your turn.

The Bible says as long as the earth remains seed time and harvest shall not cease.. Every singular action we put up is like a seed sown and very soon it would germinate and begin to yield its fruits in return back unto us. Because whatsoever a man sows, the same shall he reap and often times in multiple folds. Always remember the golden rule, "Do unto others as you would want them to do unto you". Receive grace to do right in Jesus Name.

PRAYERS FOR THE DAY

* Divine grace and Power to die to self, fall upon my life in the name of Jesus! in Jesus Name.

* I shall have a good reward for my labor on earth in Jesus name.

EXTRA RESOURCES FOR READING
Mathew 7:1-End., Luke 6:1-End., Ephesians 6:1-4

Giving Thanks for:---

I'm Praying for:---

Devotional Reflections On My Heart Today :-----------------------------------
----

Things I'm Still Struggling With :---

DAY 39
BEHOLD I AM THE GOD OF ALL FLESH
Jeremiah 32: 26-27
MEMORY VERSE

Behold, I am the LORD, the God of all flesh: is there anything too hard for me? Jeremiah 32:27 Kjv

EXPOSITION

In Genesis 18:14, God told Abraham this same phrase he told Prophet Jeremiah in the passage above "Is there anything too hard for God to do"?. Going by human natural reproductive ability, Abraham's Sarah could by no means conceive anymore. God, the manufacturer of the human body system had to reiterate that to Abraham, just in case he has forgotten, that the master of the universe is the one that's talking to him.

At the time of life, he said he would return unto Abraham and his wife Sarah would give birth to a Son by whose name he shall be called and that was exactly what happened. In Jeremiah 32:17, the prophet further emphasized the awesomeness of our God when he said "Ah Lord GOD! behold, thou hast made the heaven and the earth by thy great power and stretched out arm, and there is nothing too hard for thee".

Beloved!, God has not created anyone that he cannot arrest, he has not created anyone he cannot subdue. God has not created any mountain he cannot bring down and he has not created any power he cannot shut down. There is no situation that our God cannot dismantle, no problem that he cannot solve. He has not created you in order for him to abandon you if truly you are on his side. Hold onto him tightly, he'll not fail you.

PRAYERS FOR THE DAY

*Oh God my father, do not tarry before you settle my case in the name of Jesus

*Lord turn my impossibilities to possibilities in Jesus Name.

EXTRA RESOURCES FOR READING
Genesis 18:1-End., Mathew 21: 18-22

Giving Thanks for:--

I'm Praying for:--

Devotional Reflections On My Heart Today :--

Things I'm Still Struggling With :---

----------------------   --

DAY 40
THERE ARE THINGS GOD WILL NOT DO
James 4:1-4
MEMORY VERSE
You ask and do not receive, because you ask wrongly,
to spend it on your passions. James 4:3 Esv
EXPOSITION
There is no prayer that God cannot answer and there's no problem that God cannot solve. However, there are many prayers he WILL NOT answer and there are many problems that he will not solve. Yeah!! You heard me right!! The passage referenced above in James 4:3 says that "you ask, and you do not receive because you pray amiss in order to consume it upon your lusts". That's one of the many reasons why he won't answer a lot of prayer points until you begin to pray aright. Many times, people ask for things with selfish ulterior motives.

Hannah goes to Shiloh every year and her only prayer request was to have a son probably so she too can use the child to boast and show off like her rival Peninnah in the home. Remember their husband always gave Peninnah multiple portions for the number of her children while Hannah only gets double portion. However, the very year she changed the motive behind her prayers as recorded in 1 Samuel 1:11, the heavens noticed her and granted her request instantly.

After that the Bible recorded she also had other sons and daughters apart from Samuel. Beloved, God is ever ready to hear and respond, if only you'll change your motives and ask aright. Remember! He is the God of all flesh, there's nothing too hard for him to do. May the lord hear your voice and answer speedily in Jesus Name!.

PRAYERS FOR THE DAY
* By the Power in the blood of Jesus, my own will not be hard for the lord to do in the Name of Jesus

*Every power delaying the manifestation of my own breakthrough and testimony, release me now in the name of Jesus.

EXTRA RESOURCES FOR READING
Mathew 7: 1-7., 1 Samuel 1: 1-20

Giving Thanks for:--

I'm Praying for:--

Devotional Reflections On My Heart Today :---

Things I'm Still Struggling With :---

AM I WINNING THE RACE?
2 Timothy 4:7 - 8.

MEMORY VERSE

I returned, and saw under the sun, that the race is not to the swift, nor the battle to the strong, neither yet bread to the wise, nor yet riches to men of understanding, nor yet favor to men of skill; but time and chance happeneth to them all. Ecclesiastes 9:11Kjv

EXPOSITION

What is a Race?. A race is a competition for speed as in running or riding. It is a steady or rapid onward movement. It is to compete in a contest of speed. It is to move rapidly or at top speed in comparison to others at the same time. The Christian journey on the way to our heavenly home can be likened to this kind of athletic race in which case all are running but only a few would make it to that home.

The Bible says in Mathew 7: 13-14 that " Enter ye in at the strait gate: for wide is the gate, and broad is the way, that leadeth to destruction, and many there be which go therein: Because strait is the gate, and narrow is the way, which leadeth unto life, and few there be that find it". Entering through the narrow gate is to follow the way of the cross, practicing the old time Christianity. Not this modern day, bread and butter religion that gives excuses for compromise.

Therefore, If as a Christian, you cannot boldly say that if you drop dead today you are going to win the race, then you need to check yourself and go and make the necessary amends before it is too late because our God is not a respecter of persons. Whatsoever a man sows, that shall he also reap. The time to repent and turn to God is now.

PRAYERS FOR THE DAY

*By the Power in the blood of Jesus, I shall not fall by the wayside on this Christian journey in the name of Jesus!

*Lord help me to run this race successfully in Jesus Name.

EXTRA RESOURCES FOR READING

1 Corinthians 9:24-27., Hebrews 12: 1 - End

Giving Thanks for:---

I'm Praying for:---

Devotional Reflections On My Heart Today :---

Things I'm Still Struggling With :--

FIGHT THE GOOD FIGHT OF FAITH
1 Timothy 6:8-12
MEMORY VERSE
Fight the good fight of the faith. Take hold of the eternal life to which you were called and about which you made the good confession in the presence of many witnesses. 1Timothy 6:12Esv
EXPOSITION
Apostle Paul said in 2 Timothy 4: 7 - 8 that "I have fought a good fight, I have finished my course, I have kept the faith: Henceforth there is laid up for me a crown of righteousness, which the Lord, the righteous judge, shall give me at that day: and not to me only, but unto all them also that love his appearing. If you cannot say with boldness exactly what is said here in this passage, then, there's much work you still need to do on yourself.

The Bible commands you to "Work out your salvation with fear and trembling". The erroneous doctrine of once saved eternally saved even when it's obvious the person is living in sin would not be there to deliver anyone from hell on that day. Some think they are still on their way to heaven, when they have actually left the heavenly trail many years ago.

They have compromised the faith somewhere along the line and because their conscience doesn't trouble them anymore, they begin to think all is ok after all God understands. It would be a disastrous event, if on the last day you find out that you have missed it at certain points in your Christian journey and there's no space for you with the lord. Always examine yourself daily if you are still in the faith and I pray the lord enables you to reach your heavenly goal in Jesus name.

PRAYERS FOR THE DAY
* By the Power in the blood of Jesus, I shall not fall by the wayside on this Christian journey in the name of Jesus!

*Every power fighting my peace release me and die in Jesus name.

EXTRA RESOURCES FOR READING
2 Corinthians 13:1-7., 1 Thessalonians 5:14-End

Giving Thanks for:---

I'm Praying for:---

Devotional Reflections On My Heart Today :-------------------------------------
----

Things I'm Still Struggling With :---

------------------------   ---

DAY 43
YOU SHALL RECOVER ALL
1 Samuel 30:18-19.
MEMORY VERSE

And I will restore to you the years that the locust hath eaten, the cankerworm, and the caterpiller, and the palmerworm, my great army which I sent among you. Joel 2:25Kjv

EXPOSITION

In the book of 1 Samuel 30, David has just been plundered and robbed of everything he and his subjects had by the Amalekites. He came back and saw what the enemy has done and he wept bitterly with his followers and eventually summoned courage to ask the lord what to do. The lord gave him the assurance that he would pursue them, overtake them and that he would recover all and it did happen exactly as the lord told him it would.

David recovered all that was stolen from him without suffering any further casualty or loss in the battle. The lord is telling us here as his children that if only we would trust him enough to ask for directions in our daily pursuit for recovery and restoration, we would definitely recover all. If he did it for David, he'll surely do it for us.

The Bible says in Psalms 126: 1 "that when the Lord turned again the captivity of Zion, we were like them that dream". By the time the lost glory of yesteryears are restored, it would be as if you are in a trance because it totally becomes unbelievable even to you that's experiencing the testimony. That's going to be the wow experience. Stay in tune with God. Hope's not yet lost because Help is on the way.

PRAYERS FOR THE DAY

* The power to pursue, to overtake and to recover all the enemy has stolen, come upon me today in the name of Jesus!

*Oh lord arise and frustrate every evil power opposing my time and season of greatness in the name of Jesus.

EXTRA RESOURCES FOR READING
Psalms 126:1 - End., Mathew 7: 1-8., Joel 2: 1-End

Giving Thanks for:--

I'm Praying for:--

Devotional Reflections On My Heart Today :----------------------------------

----

Things I'm Still Struggling With :--

DAY 44
AND THIS TOO SHALL PASS
Jeremiah 30:15-20
MEMORY VERSE
For I will restore health to you, and your wounds I will heal, declares the Lord, because they have called you an outcast: It is Zion, for whom no one cares! Jeremiah 30:17Esv

EXPOSITION
It's possible for an individual to spend years laboring and struggling just to get by, and no matter how hard they try, it just seem as if their lives keeps going backward. It's like they are sick spiritually and everything seems to be against them because they have nothing to show for all the years of work. They now feel the enemy has succeeded in wasting their years.

Sometimes, it's possible for someone to begin to think he/she is failing simply because everything or most things they lay their hands upon to do, always ends in total disaster or defeat and right now are at the verge of giving up or even about committing suicide. To them, it's like the locust and cankerworm and every devourer known to man deliberately singled them out for attack, and they don't even know the way out.

If that is your situation or maybe you know someone like that, then that passage in Jeremiah 30:17 above is for you. Don't wonder too much, this is an issue with your foundation.. The bible says if the foundation be destroyed, what can the righteous do? Beloved, the righteous can pray. Go to God in prayers and ask for healing because obviously your land is sick and just like Prophet Elisha spoke to the land of Jericho in 2 kings 2:21 and the land was healed, the lord is would restore perfect health unto you and it shall pass in Jesus name.

PRAYERS FOR THE DAY
* I recover back all my wasted years in the Name of Jesus
* I shall not labor in vain in my lifetime in the name of Jesus.

EXTRA RESOURCES FOR READING
Job 42:10-17., Jeremiah 29:12-13

Giving Thanks for:---

I'm Praying for:---

Devotional Reflections On My Heart Today :--

Things I'm Still Struggling With :---

----------------------------- ---
--- --

DAY 45
YOUR DESTROYER SHALL BE DESTROYED
Zechariah 4:4-10.
MEMORY VERSE
Behold, I am against thee, O destroying mountain, saith the Lord, which destroyest all the earth: and I will stretch out mine hand upon thee, and roll thee down from the rocks, and will make thee a burnt mountain. Jeremiah 51:25(Kjv)

EXPOSITION
The word of the lord to you today is this "Any destroying mountain standing before you on the way to your testimony shall be destroyed in the name of Jesus". The lord spoke to Zerubbabel saying it's not by power not by might but by the spirit of the lord So quit trying to climb that mountain all by your own power, quit trying to destroy that mountain by your own strength because the Bible says by strength shall no man prevail.

Remember in Exodus 15:8 it is written "By the blast of your nostrils the waters piled up. The surging waters stood up like a wall; the deep waters congealed in the heart of the sea". Our God is the one who sits in the heavenlies and rules over the affairs of men, he is the master of the universe. At a rebuke from him the surging waves of the sea calmed down.

He spoke to the fig tree that no one eats of its fruits again and the fig tree withered. When you allow him to ride upon your mountain, the mountain crumbles into powder. When he speaks unto your mountain, the mountain breaks down into pieces and you'll pick up the headstone to show as a testimony of what the lord has done. Receive victory this day in Jesus Name.

PRAYERS FOR THE DAY
*Every destroying mountain standing against my life, be destroyed by fire in the name of Jesus!

*I receive victory over every unfavorable situation in Jesus name.

EXTRA RESOURCES FOR READING
Jeremiah 30:16-20., Psalms 18:1-End., Zechariah 4:4-10

Giving Thanks for:---

I'm Praying for:---

Devotional Reflections On My Heart Today :------------------------------------
----

Things I'm Still Struggling With :---

---------------------   --

CONFRONT YOUR FEARS
Psalms 118:6-9
MEMORY VERSE
The LORD is on my side; I will not fear. What can man do to me? Psalms 118:6 Nkjv
EXPOSITION

It's natural for man to experience fear at some points during their lifetime but problem comes when someone begins to exhibit fear over just anything and over things that obviously do not exist, like the unknown. And that's absolutely a fact. Many people are living in the fear of the unknown. They worry about what lies ahead of them in the future and how they would handle them. Beloved, why should you die before your time. Don't you know that fear has torment?

What the devil is trying to do is to destroy you with that spirit of fear and as a child of God, you need to stand your ground and tell the enemy to take his dirty hand off your mind and your life. It's time for you to confront those fears and eliminate the destroyer. In Psalms 9:6a, the lord says "Oh thou enemy, destructions have come to a perpetual end" the lord is putting an end to every activity of the destructive enemy in your life today and that destructive enemy in your life shall be destroyed in the name of Jesus.

In the book of Jeremiah 30:17, the bible says "Therefore all they that devour thee shall be devoured; and all thine adversaries, every one of them, shall go into captivity; and they that spoil thee shall be a spoil, and all that prey upon thee will I give for a prey". That spirit of fear is simply trying to destroy you, but God is saying he will destroy that Destroying Mountain standing before you and you shall glorify him in Jesus Name.

PRAYERS FOR THE DAY

* Every activity of the destroyer in my life, cease by fire in the Name of Jesus!

* Every situation tormenting my life, release me now in Jesus name

EXTRA RESOURCES FOR READING
Jeremiah 51:19-26., Psalms 9:1-End., John 14:26-28

Giving Thanks for:--

I'm Praying for:---

Devotional Reflections On My Heart Today :------------------------------------

----

Things I'm Still Struggling With :--

DAY 47
THE CHOICE IS YOURS
Proverbs 6:10-12
MEMORY VERSE

Seest thou a man diligent in his business? he shall stand before kings; he shall not stand before mean men. Proverbs 22:29 Kjv

EXPOSITION

The lord has given man the power of choice that's why he allows you to decide what you want from life. The desire of every human being is to prosper and to live in affluence and It is equally the wish of the lord also for you to live in prosperity. He said in 3 John:2 that "Beloved, I wish above all things that you may prosper and be in health, even as your soul prospers ".

Unfortunately, not everyone will prosper, because some chose either consciously or unconsciously not to prosper. There are conditions that must be fulfilled for God's kind of prosperity to come into someone's life. It is not automatic, otherwise everyone would be living in affluence. The bible says poor people would always be on earth, but you don't have to be among those poor, and you get to make that choice on your own.

First, you must make up your mind that you want to prosper and choose not to settle for anything less than prosperity. Secondly, you must take conscious steps towards prosperity by following biblical principles on the law of Sowing and reaping mentioned in the book of Genesis 8:22, tithing in Malachi 3:8-12 and thirdly, the positive use of your tongue mentioned in Proverbs 18:21. If you do not apply the three principles together along with strategic and prosperity provoking prayers, then prosperity might remain a wish that couldn't be realized.

PRAYERS FOR THE DAY

*Anointing and Power for prosperity fall upon my life in Jesus name
*Lord I need your guidance in the choices I make in Jesus name.

EXTRA RESOURCES FOR READING
Malachi 3:8-12., Genesis 8: 1-22., Proverbs 18:1-End

Giving Thanks for:--

I'm Praying for:--

Devotional Reflections On My Heart Today :------------------------------------
----

Things I'm Still Struggling With :--

------------------------   --

DAY 48
ENTER NOT INTO BABYLON WHILE IN ZION
Psalms 24:1-6.
MEMORY VERSE
Who shall ascend into the hill of the Lord? or who shall stand in his holy place? He that hath clean hands, and a pure heart; who hath not lifted up his soul unto vanity, nor sworn deceitfully. Psalm 24: 3-4 Kjv

EXPOSITION
There are several ways by which a Christian can enter into Babylon while in Zion. The first is when you fail to remember that your salvation and deliverance are personal things and begin to rate your Christian race by earthly standards rather than the standards set forth in the scriptures. Also, when you fail to stick to your first decision for God, but instead you are now only looking for what you can get from God rather than what you can do for God instead.

By the time you as a Christian start becoming unfaithful to God in little things, you can no longer pay your tithe as an act of obedience, but it becomes an obligation. The Bible is now far from your heart but instead has only become a mere book in your hand and to study God's word is now a burden for you to do. When As a child of God when you have become so prayerless and living a sinful life is now a normal thing to you and your heart no longer convicts you when you sin.

Beloved!, If you have any of these and many more like them in your life, then you are already living in Babylon while thinking you are in Zion. The lord is calling you to repentance now because tomorrow may be too late. Your reading this now may be the only opportunity you'll have to change. The time to do it right is now.

PRAYERS FOR THE DAY
*Every power dragging me to Hell Fire, release me and die in the name of Jesus.

*Lord release your fresh fire, quicken my spirit man in Jesus name.

EXTRA RESOURCES FOR READING
Psalms 137: 1 - End., Micah 6: 1-8., 1 John 2: 1-End

MY JOURNAL FOR TODAY / /20____

Giving Thanks for:--

I'm Praying for:---

Devotional Reflections On My Heart Today :-------------------------------------
----

Things I'm Still Struggling With :---

------------------------ ---

CAPTURED BY THE ENEMY
2 Kings 25:1-7
MEMORY VERSE
Watch and pray that you may not enter into temptation. The spirit indeed is willing, but the flesh is weak. Mark 14:38 Esv

EXPOSITION
In 2 Kings 25:1, Nebuchadnezzar, king of Babylon besieged Jerusalem for 6 months until there was so much famine in the land and the people of Jerusalem gave up and were taken into captivity. The king "Zedekiah" was captured, and all his children killed before his eyes. This story tells us that as Christians to constantly be sober and vigilant because the enemy stands around the corner and lay siege everyday seeking whom he may devour and destroy (1 Peter 5:8).

He throws his darts of temptations and trials to make us fall into sin/compromise. He does not give up until his target succumb to his antics and pressure and that gives him the legal ground to wreak havoc in such a life. As a Christian, when you feel the pressure from within to succumb to the pleasures which your eyes are seeing, then it's time to go consciously in the opposite direction because that's the devil pressuring you. If you let off your guards and become weak, the enemy comes in and introduce one form or captivity or another into your life.

As a child of God, you must stand firm and hold fast unto that which you have so the enemy does not steal your freedom of salvation and therefore capture you into eternal damnation. May the lord empower you to defeat the enemy and overcome in Jesus name.

PRAYERS FOR THE DAY
*The grace to do thorough self-examination and the power to effect the right changes, fall upon me in Jesus Name.

*Power to stand my ground against the enemy, fall upon me in the name of Jesus.

EXTRA RESOURCES FOR READING
Psalm 12:1-End., 1 Kings 25:1 - End., Philippians 2:1-End

Giving Thanks for:--

I'm Praying for:--

Devotional Reflections On My Heart Today :--

Things I'm Still Struggling With :---

DAY 50
STRANGE STORMS ARE DEFEATABLE
Mathew 14:22-32.
MEMORY VERSE
I have said these things to you, that in me you may have peace. In the world, you will have tribulation. But take heart; I have overcome the world. John 16:33Kjv

EXPOSITION
There are lots of questions in life that we cannot answer until the day we see God in heaven. When a person is experiencing storms, it means the atmospheric condition of that life is disturbed. Storms are strange, because they are not things you desire but they manipulate you against your heart desire.

Whatever situations you find yourself, you need to thank the lord. A lot of times, we fast and pray about issues and yet nothing happens because there is a storm behind the situation. The person you discuss your life with may be the problem or the padlock behind the problems in your life. Whenever there is a storm in any life, what you notice is that in most cases such a life would be stagnant. That storm might likely keep the person perpetually at that particular level.

In Acts 3:1-10, the situation here crippled this man, people carry him around and he couldn't do anything without the help of people. This storm kept him at that spot for a very long time. The only help they could do for him is to give him money, but one day there was a change because weeping may endure for a night, but joy comes in the morning. Remember you serve a God who is master over storms of life. He's always there for you.

PRAYERS FOR THE DAY
* Every strange storm tormenting my life, release me and die in the name of Jesus

* Holy ghost fire incubate me from strange powers that are stronger than me in the name of Jesus.

EXTRA RESOURCES FOR READING
Acts 3:1-10., 2 Corinthians 4:8-9., Isaiah 43:1-2

Giving Thanks for:---

I'm Praying for:---

Devotional Reflections On My Heart Today :------------------------------------
----

Things I'm Still Struggling With :---

DAY 51
HE WILL PICK YOU UP
Isaiah 43:1-5

MEMORY VERSE

When you pass through the waters, I will be with you; and through the rivers, they shall not overwhelm you; when you walk through fire you shall not be burned, and the flame shall not consume you. Isaiah 43:2 Esv

EXPOSITION

Dearly beloved, do not be dismayed when people disappoint you and they decide to cut off from you for no just cause. Know for a fact that until they drop you, God cannot pick you up. You heard me right beloved. Until all the people you look up to for help disappoint you, until they desert you and all your humanly arranged help and alternatives have failed, God cannot pick you up, because his glory he would not share with any man.

So, when people disappoint you, know that God is busy packaging something better and more superior for you. Are you afraid of someone not helping you anymore?, wait for your God. It is only the person whom God has sent to you that cannot disappoint you, so don't take it against them. Just know that it's either their part to play in your life is over or that God has a better plan for you, and he wants to pick you up.

Are you currently facing strange storms and are looking up to man for help? Quit looking but focus on Jesus. In Mathew 14, Peter shifted his focus from Jesus, and he began to sink. Jesus had to rush to his rescue to keep him from perishing in the storm. Keep your focus on him and if you don't doubt his abilities, he'll rescue you.

PRAYERS FOR THE DAY

* Every secret weapon the enemy is using to punish me, holy ghost fire, destroy them in the name of Jesus

* I shall not be destroyed on the battlefield of life in Jesus name.

EXTRA RESOURCES FOR READING
Isaiah 41:1-10., Mathew 28:16-20., John 14:25-28

Giving Thanks for: --

I'm Praying for: --

Devotional Reflections On My Heart Today : --

Things I'm Still Struggling With : --

DAY 52
TIME AND CHANCE
Ecclesiastes 9:1-End.
MEMORY VERSE

Again I saw that under the sun the race is not to the swift, nor the battle to the strong, nor bread to the wise, nor riches to the intelligent, nor favor to those with knowledge, but time and chance happen to them all. Ecclesiastes 9:11 Esv

EXPOSITION

Time and Opportunity or Chance is a really terrible thing to waste but sadly enough, those are some of the very things that people waste in life and it often takes a very long time before people get to realize how much of life's opportunities they have wasted or passed by. There's a popular saying that an opportunity once lost may never be regained. It's important for everyone to make the best use of every available chance that life throws our way.

Some find this out much later in life when it's already too late to do anything about it, while some are fortunate enough to realize it early enough and are able to salvage it really quickly. Ecclesiastes 9:11 tells us that it's not about how smart you are that guarantees success in life, but that successful people are children of time and opportunities.

It is often said that in the lifetime of an individual, there's always at least one chance at success but it's up to you to make use of it or to pass it over. The book of Ecclesiastes 10:7 says, "I have seen servants upon horses, and princes walking as servants upon the earth". This happens because the servant seized an opportunity that the prince failed to see or utilize. May you not miss your own lifetime opportunity at success in the name of Jesus.

PRAYERS FOR THE DAY

* Oh lord, open my eyes to see the opportunities around me that would usher me into greatness in the name of Jesus

* Anointing for divine speed, fall upon me in the name of Jesus.

EXTRA RESOURCES FOR READING
1 Samuel 17:45-54., Psalms 20:1- End., Psalms 33:16

Giving Thanks for:---

I'm Praying for:---

Devotional Reflections On My Heart Today :--

Things I'm Still Struggling With :---

----------------------- ---

DAY 53
YOU SHALL FINISH WELL
Ecclesiastes 7:7-10
MEMORY VERSE
Better is the end of a thing than the beginning thereof: and the patient in spirit is better than the proud in spirit. Eccl.7:8Kjv
EXPOSITION
Life is a journey and everyone is in a race, but if you think you are intelligent or smart and are too confident in your abilities, don't be so sure of success, because circumstances around may make you lose the race and the winning prize goes to even the less qualified because chance permitted them. That's why for a Christian, asking for divine assistance cannot be traded for anything on earth. If God helps you, then all that you need to finish well would be made available to you.

I watched the Olympic games a few years back in which the best and most favored athlete in the competition pulled a hamstring just when he was close to the finish line, only for the least able competitor to end up as the winner. Likewise, many run in a race but don't finish well because situations and unexpected circumstances worked against them. Beloved, pray to finish well in this Christian race

In Romans 9:16 the bible says, "So then it is not of him that willeth, nor of him that runneth, but of God that showeth mercy". As a Christian, it doesn't glorify God to end your journey as the loser. Therefore, you need to ask the lord to give you the power to run your life's race and Christian race with excellence in everything. I pray that the power and grace to finish well in all you do will come upon you today in the name of Jesus.

PRAYERS FOR THE DAY
*By the power in the blood of Jesus, I receive power and grace to finish well in my journey and undertakings in Jesus Name.

*Let the mercy of God show up for me every day in Jesus name.

EXTRA RESOURCES FOR READING
2 Chronicles 18:33 - 34., 1 Corinthians 9:24-27., Acts 20:24

Giving Thanks for:---

I'm Praying for:---

Devotional Reflections On My Heart Today :-----------------------------------
----

Things I'm Still Struggling With :--

DAY 54
DISEASE IS NOT YOUR PORTION
Isaiah 53:1-7.
MEMORY VERSE
But he was wounded for our transgressions, he was bruised for our iniquities: the chastisement of our peace was upon him; and with his stripes we are healed. Isaiah 53:5Kjv

EXPOSITION
Beloved, I don't know the kind of infirmity that is in your body at the moment. Maybe yours is an emotional sickness or maybe yours is a spiritual ailment that has defied every scientific or medical explanation. Jesus is still in the business of healing and restoration. He is the master of the universe and there are no impossibilities with him for those who believe because it is written, all things are possible to those who believe (Mark 9:23)

It is possible that you might be sick financially and you don't even know how or where you are headed at the moment. That also is his specialty. He's knows how to fix that. If in the midst of a terrible famine, when all hope was lost, he still prospered the widow of Zarephath, then he is able to cause a positive turn around in that business. Or do you feel that something is wrong with your foundation and you believe it's a foundational sickness. He can fix that too.

Remember, he healed the foundation of that city of Jericho through his Servant "Prophet Elisha"'. Then yours is not hard for him to do. He would surely heal your land. All it requires now is a little faith as tiny as that size of a Mustard seed and you'll surely become a testifier to his goodness. Remember all things are Possible to them that believe. Only believe, and you'll see the salvation of the Lord.

PRAYERS FOR THE DAY
* I curse every root and seed of infirmity in my body and I command that infirmities to die in the name of Jesus!

* Arrows of disease in my life, release me and die in Jesus name

EXTRA RESOURCES FOR READING
Exodus 15:22-27., Psalms 147:2-12., Acts 10:36-39

Giving Thanks for:--

I'm Praying for:---

Devotional Reflections On My Heart Today :--

Things I'm Still Struggling With :--

----------------------------   --
--- --

DAY 55
ARE YOU SERVING GOD OR MONEY [Part 1]?
Exodus 20:3-5
MEMORY VERSE
Thou shalt have no other gods before me. Exodus 20:3 Kjv
EXPOSITION
Why do people wake up in the morning and head out to work? Very Simple answer!!. Beloved! It is Money. That's why the Bible says in Ecclesiastes 10:19 that Money answers all things. Maybe you're one of those who have said before that money is the root of all evil. Well, let me quickly correct that now. Ecclesiastes 7:12 says that Money is a defense. Our God himself told us through his word in the book of Haggai 2:8 that the Silver and the Gold are his.

This means that Money in itself is not evil, but the inordinate pursuit and love of it is the evil therein. Money becomes an evil thing when we love it to the point that we place the pursuit of money ahead of God. At that point money has replaced God in our lives and has invariably become another God. In 1 Timothy 6:10, it is written "For the love of money is the root of all evil: which while some coveted after, they have erred from the faith, and pierced themselves through with many sorrows."

Whatever makes anyone to go and kill or destroy another person's reputation when in competition for the same thing is no other thing but the love of Money. Or what would make a beautiful young lady to go and be sleeping around in exchange for cash if not the love of Money?. If you have ever done any of these or have placed money ahead of God, then you need to repent and return to him today.

PRAYERS FOR THE DAY
*By the power in the name of Jesus, the pursuit of material wealth shall not send me to Hell Fire in Jesus name

*Every covetous spirit in my life, release me now in Jesus name

EXTRA RESOURCES FOR READING
Ecclesiastes 10:1-End., Ecclesiastes 5: 1-End., Psalms 39:1-6

Giving Thanks for:---

I'm Praying for:---

Devotional Reflections On My Heart Today :-------------------------------------
----

Things I'm Still Struggling With :---

DAY 56
ARE YOU SERVING GOD OR MONEY [Part 2]?
Ecclesiastes 5:8-16
MEMORY VERSE
He who loves money will not be satisfied with money, nor he who loves wealth with his income; this also is vanity. Ecclesiastes 5:10 Esv

EXPOSITION
Ok! Let's consider a situation where it is time for Sunday worship, then, you get a call to come and work for extra pay at the same time. If what you do is choose the extra cash over your fellowship with God? then money has become your god. How do you explain the prayerlessness in your life when every morning, after you wake up you never have a quiet time to fellowship with God in devotion, but instead you are always in a rush to get out to work so as not to be late.

A lot of Christians have quietly chosen the God of Money over the almighty God and they do not even know it. Their initial love for God has suddenly waxed cold and they think they are still very much in the faith. Some have become strangers to their beds because it's from one job to another 24/7, all in the pursuit of material wealth. You must know that it is the blessings of the lord that makes rich and adds no sorrow to it.

The lord wants you to prosper without sweat, he wants money to follow you on its own. Psalms 39:6 says, "Surely everyone goes around like a mere phantom; in vain they rush about, heaping up wealth without knowing whose it will finally be". So, the question to ask yourself today is this... "WHO AM I SERVING? GOD OR MONEY? I pray the lord would help you to do the right thing in Jesus Name.

PRAYERS FOR THE DAY
*Oh God my father, help me to be focused on you and be dead to the inordinate affection for vanity in the Name of Jesus.

*Oh lord, help me to outgrow my weaknesses in Jesus name.

EXTRA RESOURCES FOR READING
1 Timothy 6:1-End., Ecclesiastes 8:1-End., Haggai 2:1-End.

Giving Thanks for:--

I'm Praying for:---

Devotional Reflections On My Heart Today :---------------------------------
----

Things I'm Still Struggling With :--

--------------------------   --

DAY 57
JEHOVAH GAVE ALL
John 3:16-18
MEMORY VERSE
For God so love the world that he gave his only begotten son, that whosoever believes in him should not perish but have eternal life. John 3:16 Nkjv

EXPOSITION
Our God so love humanity that he chose to give us all what he has "HIS SON" Jesus Christ. The question is, "what are you giving to him in return". As children of God, it is time for us to put an end to Bread and Butter Christianity and think about what we can give in return to the lord.

As a Christian, you need to know that the only way your mansion in heaven would be ready by the time you get there would depend on how much you have given back to him in terms of your time, resources and labor spent in his service, caring for believers and unbelievers alike and working in his vineyard.

The Bible says every work would be tested with fire, So, the question I want to ask you today is this: When your labor and work is tested with fire, will it go up in flames or will it stand the test and come out shining better as Gold. God is looking for people who would give the totality of themselves to him so he can prepare them and make them useful in his end time army for the harvesting of souls for eternity in heaven. The question for you now is this: Are you ready and available?

Beloved, when you are working for God, he would be working for you. Things would be working for you without any efforts on your part. May you be found worthy of service for the lord in Jesus Name.

PRAYERS FOR THE DAY
*The grace to be available as a faithful laborer for you in this end time, oh lord release it upon me in Jesus Name.

* Lord empower me for service to you and humanity in Jesus name.

EXTRA RESOURCES FOR READING
1 John 4:9-11., Romans 8:37-39., John 15:9-17

Giving Thanks for: ---

I'm Praying for: ---

Devotional Reflections On My Heart Today : --------------------------------------
----

Things I'm Still Struggling With : --

--------------------------   --

ALL THINGS FOR JESUS
Genesis 1:12-17

MEMORY VERSE
For by him all things were created, in heaven and on earth, visible and invisible, whether thrones or dominions or rulers or authorities all things were created through him and for him. Colossians 1:16 Esv

EXPOSITION
The Bible makes it clear that all things, both visible and invisible, tangible and intangible, were created by, for, and through Jesus Christ. From the beginning, He made all things good, bright, and beautiful (Gen. 1:12, 17; Jn. 1:1-3). All people of all races, tradition and culture must be treated the same (Gal. 3:28). God sees good in everything and in all people, no matter their circumstances, places, or positions (Jer.29:11).

Before the fall, Man saw the woman as the bone of his bones. If that is still so, why then do we have battery and divorce in homes, today? Why are pastors, elders and members not able to work together in some churches? Have we changed from that beautiful man/woman God made us? As God's children, our attitudes must pattern after Christ, the full image of the Father.

You must also know that, all that we are and have, are His, and so, must be used for him. This same Jesus who came to die on the cross and save humanity, is coming to judge humanity and put everyone where he/she belongs – heaven, or hell. Therefore, live your life for his glory and with Him here, do what is right because he's taking account, so that you can reign with Him in eternity.

PRAYERS FOR THE DAY
* Father lord,, ignite my spirit with your revival fire, so I may stand firm in you in the name of Jesus.

* Lord, arise and do what you alone can do in my life in Jesus name.

EXTRA RESOURCES FOR READING
Ecclesiastes 3:9-13., Job 12:7-9., Psalm 8:1-9

Giving Thanks for:---

I'm Praying for:--

Devotional Reflections On My Heart Today :------------------------------------

----

Things I'm Still Struggling With :---

NEW BEGINNING
Isaiah 43:19-21.
MEMORY VERSE
Behold, I will do a new thing; now it shall spring forth; shall ye not know it? I will even make a way in the wilderness, and rivers in the desert. Isaiah 43:19 Nkjv

EXPOSITION
Every person on this planet would at certain point in life have something referred to as "the wilderness experience." It is a period when a person is at his/her lowest point and it seems as if they are just wondering about, not knowing what to do or which way to go or how to proceed. The same situations was faced by the Israelites after they left Egypt for the promised land.

The lord promised taking them to the promised land, but he didn't tell them what they'll pass through before they get there. Likewise, for children of God today, when in that situation. How long a person stays in that wilderness situation will depend on attitude and how much of God is allowed in during the time. Maybe that is your situation at this time , then, quit trying to do it by your own wisdom, just surrender it all to the lord and you'll begin to see him walk you through that wilderness, carrying you on his wings.

Do not be like the Israelites who complained and grumbled, and they all perished in the wilderness. Believe on the lord who can carry you through and you'll come out victorious. Do not give up, he'll see you through and you would give testimony. Help is on the way. He is the God of new beginning and he'll do a new thing if you'll let him.

PRAYERS FOR THE DAY
*By the power in the blood of Jesus, I shall not perish in the wilderness of life, I shall overcome in Jesus Name.

*God of new beginning begin a new thing in my life in Jesus name.

EXTRA RESOURCES FOR READING
1 Kings 19:1-9., Proverbs 3:5-6., Exodus 15:22-26

Giving Thanks for:---

I'm Praying for:--

Devotional Reflections On My Heart Today :-------------------------------------

----

Things I'm Still Struggling With :---

DAY 60
IT IS POSSIBLE
Mark 9:23-27.
MEMORY VERSE
Jesus said to him, "If you can believe, all things are possible to him who believes. Mark 9:23 Nkjv

EXPOSITION

Jesus was talking to the father of a boy which had the dumb spirit here. His disciples could not cast out the spirit in the boy and here we see Jesus referring to them as a faithless generation. Jesus was trying to make a point here and teach us a very important lesson, that all it requires is for us as Christians of this generation to just have a tiny bit of faith believing that the thing we desire is possible to come true and that tiny faith like that of a mustard seed would make it happen for us.

The mustard seed is the smallest of all seeds, even tinier than a small pin head. However, there's assurance that if that seed gets into the ground and touches water, it grows into the biggest of all trees on earth. That's just the kind of faith it takes to excel, that's how much faith God requires you to have for you to achieve your purpose in life and secure that your much-desired goal.

Whatever it is that you are trusting the lord for, all it takes is just for you to keep your mind focused on God and if you do not doubt in your heart, you'll have it. God is not a man that he should lie. Only have an unwavering faith that he's able to do as he said. Believe it!! It is possible!! You can achieve it!! You will get there, because all things are possible to them that believes.

PRAYERS FOR THE DAY

* Every power that wants me to struggle till I die, Oh, you ground, open up and swallow them in the Name of Jesus.

* Oh lord arise and turn around every impossibility in my life into testimonies in the name of Jesus.

EXTRA RESOURCES FOR READING
Mathew 17:20-24., Mark 11:22-24., Hebrews 11:1-39

Giving Thanks for:---

I'm Praying for:--

Devotional Reflections On My Heart Today :-----------------------------------
----

Things I'm Still Struggling With :--

--------------------   ---

DAY 61
FEAR NOT
Psalms 23: 4-6

MEMORY VERSE

"Yea, though I walk through the valley of the shadow of death, I will fear no evil: for thou art with me; thy rod and thy staff they comfort me." Psalms 23:4 Kjv

EXPOSITION

One of the greatest weapons the devil uses against believers today is FEAR. People are constantly afraid of what lies ahead, The fear of the unknown is killing lots of people silently, fear of the enemy, fear of something terrible happening all of a sudden, fear of going broke, fear of death, fear of failing and so on and so forth.

However, the Bible says in 1 John 4:15b that "fear has torment, but perfect love cast out all fears". That's why the lord gave us 365 "FEAR NOT" in the scriptures meaning that there's one available for each day of the year. God wants us to look unto him every single day of the year and not to whatever the devil uses to harass us every day. He tells us not to worry about tomorrow because the trouble of each day is enough for that day.

A very popular adage says, "Cowards die many times before their death". So, do not be afraid because as long as you have Jesus in your life and he is on your side, he is in Control. Psalms 23:4 above gives us confidence that death being the greatest fear that could come upon man should not even make us afraid as children of God because God is with us and would comfort us all the way. Therefore beloved! "DO NOT FEAR".

PRAYERS FOR THE DAY

* I lay at the feet of Jesus today by faith, every source of fear and worries in my life in the name of Jesus.

* Every agent of fear and discouragement in my life, be frustrated in the Name of Jesus.

EXTRA RESOURCES FOR READING

Philippians 4:6-7., Psalms 27:1-14., Isaiah 43:2-5

Giving Thanks for:--

I'm Praying for:---

Devotional Reflections On My Heart Today :------------------------------------
----

Things I'm Still Struggling With :---

-------------------------- ---

DAY 62
WHERE WILL YOU SPEND ETERNITY
Hebrews 9: 24-28
MEMORY VERSE
"And as it is appointed for men to die once, but after this the judgment." Hebrews 9:27 Nkjv

EXPOSITION

Hmnn! Appointments!. Does that Sound familiar? I'm pretty sure lots of time you would have heard of people talking about going for an appointment, either a business appointment or other kinds of appointments. Sometimes, due to unavoidable circumstances we call to cancel or reschedule some of those appointments, either when we don't consider them important or when we just find it hard or impossible to make it to those appointments.

However, there's one appointment that everyone would have to keep someday either we like it or not. That appointment cannot be canceled or rescheduled, either you are busy or not busy, or whether you have time or don't have time, whether you must be at work or attend to family or not, you just must keep that appointment because when it's time, it's time. That appointment is DEATH.

Yes! Death is by appointment and that's why the passage above says, "IT IS APPOINTED FOR MAN TO DIE ONCE...". At that point there may not be the chance to make amends anymore because not everyone would have that chance to correct past errors and repent. It's therefore important as a person to live every day for Christ, as if it's going to be the last. I encourage you to make amends where necessary this very moment, because tomorrow may be too late.

PRAYERS FOR THE DAY

* Oh lord, help me to live for you every day of my life and to do the right things every moment in Jesus Name.

* I shall not die before my time in the name of Jesus.

EXTRA RESOURCES FOR READING
Joshua 24:14-15., John 3:14-17., Romans 6:21-23.

Giving Thanks for:--

I'm Praying for:--

Devotional Reflections On My Heart Today :----------------------------------
----

Things I'm Still Struggling With :--

---------------------- ---

DAY 63
DON'T LET SATAN STEAL YOU FOR ETERNITY
John 10:10-12
MEMORY VERSE

The thief does not come except to steal, and to kill, and to destroy. I have come that they may have life, and that they may have it more abundantly. John 10:10 Nkjv

EXPOSITION

The memory verse for today makes it clear what the plan of the enemy is for every believer and that is primarily to Steal the soul of every believer. Now, it is left for you to decide whether to let him do it and derail you for eternity or not. The Bible says, "Choose you this day whom you will serve". I encourage you to choose the lord and live for him every day, so you'll have peace in Eternity.

You have to know that, for every item the devil has on display, there is a price tag on it and the reason why the Bible says the Wages of Sin is Death. I pray we would all have a place in heaven for eternity in Jesus Name. Eternity is a really long time, and just in case you still wondering how long that is, let me quickly break it down here.

If an ant were to go from a 20-mile distance to the Beach and back, only to just pick up a grain of sand from the beach, drop it off and walk back the 20-mile again to pick up another grain. By the time the ant would finish emptying the beach of all the sand there, eternity has just started. I've heard people say, they'll get used to the fire in hell after a while. Beloved, No one ever gets used to a life of suffering, even here on earth. Examine yourself to know, whether you are still in the faith while there's still time and quickly realign yourself with God.

PRAYERS FOR THE DAY

* The Power and grace to flee from every form of sin lurking around, oh lord give unto me today in Jesus Name.

* The devil shall not steal my eternity in the name of Jesus.

EXTRA RESOURCES FOR READING
Hebrews 12:1-2., Joshua 24:14-20., 2 Corinthians 13:5-11

Giving Thanks for:---

I'm Praying for:---

Devotional Reflections On My Heart Today :---------------------------------
----

Things I'm Still Struggling With :---

--------------------   --

DAY 64
YOUR ATTITUDE
1 Samuel 2:1-4
MEMORY VERSE

"Talk no more so very proudly; Let no arrogance come from your mouth, For the Lord is the God of knowledge; And by Him actions are weighed.1 Samuel 2:3 Nkjv

EXPOSITION

Every human have an Attitude that is peculiar or unique to each person. "Attitude differs from character" and it could be negative or positive attitudes. This is a major factor that's debarring many people since the beginning of creation from reaching their God ordained destination in life. For example, the Israelites on their way to the promised land on several occasions, displayed their negative attitudes when they started complaining about things they were supposed to be enjoying like when they were in Egypt and that provoked God to anger.

For those reasons, the lord brought plagues, destruction and delays into their lives and journey. They would not have stayed that long in the wilderness but for their negative attitudes. Again, when it was time to go and spy the promised land, seven men were sent, but only Joshua and Caleb came back with the right attitude and report on what they saw. It wasn't surprising too that only the two of them made it into the promised land out of the over 2 million that left Egypt.

That's what a positive mental attitude can do to people. From the memory verse for today, we can see that God is watching every of your actions and he would judge and deal with you, based on the weight of those actions. Know for a fact that your attitude would determine your altitude. So, watch it, so it doesn't derail your destiny.

PRAYERS FOR THE DAY

* Oh lord empower me to have the right mental attitude that would not prolong hardship in my life in Jesus name.

* Oh lord deliver me from myself in the name of Jesus.

EXTRA RESOURCES FOR READING!
Numbers 11:1-15, Numbers 14: 1-15.

Giving Thanks for:--

I'm Praying for:---

Devotional Reflections On My Heart Today :-------------------------------------
----

Things I'm Still Struggling With :--

DAY 65
HOW IS YOUR CHARACTER
Romans 5:3-5
MEMORY VERSE
"And not only this, but we also exult in our tribulations, knowing that tribulation brings about perseverance; and perseverance, proven character; and proven character, hope" Romans 5:3 Nasb

EXPOSITION
"Character brings forth Action, and Actions shape Destinies." Good character is a virtue and whether you believe it or not, many people out there do not have it good in them. Many people have lost divine opportunities, many have pushed away their God ordained helpers because they lack Godly Character.

You never truly know what the true character of someone is until the right situation comes into play, then the real character will show up. And that's exactly what the scriptural passage above is talking about "Tribulation brings perseverance, and perseverance proven character. Many who appear so humble at some point, would transform into arrogant and devilish creatures when a little power or wealth gets into their hands and that's the reason why they have remained at the level they are in.

The lord knows the true content of the heart and thus would not give them what they have been requesting. The Bible says in James 4:3 "You ask and do not receive because you ask amiss in other to consume it upon your lust." Yes, because the motive behind it is bad and that boils down to character. If you manage your character properly, the future ahead remains bright.

PRAYERS FOR THE DAY
* Help me oh lord to build a positive character to affect my generation in the name of Jesus.

* Oh lord help me to be true to you, when tested in Jesus name.

EXTRA RESOURCES FOR READING
James 4:3-7., 2 Peter 1:5-7., Colossians 3:12-15

Giving Thanks for:--

I'm Praying for:--

Devotional Reflections On My Heart Today :----------------------------------
----

Things I'm Still Struggling With :--

DAY 66
GODLINESS WITH CONTENTMENT
1 Timothy 6:6-11
MEMORY VERSE

But godliness with contentment is great gain. For we brought nothing into this world, and it is certain we can carry nothing out. 1 Timothy 6:6-7 Kjv

EXPOSITION

Godliness and contentment is an attribute of Christian character. We can find many examples of this scattered throughout the scriptures for us believers to emulate. A certain woman named Ruth in the Scriptures is a fine epitome of godly character for all. Ruth who was a gentile, found herself to be in the lineage of becoming a great grandmother of the Lord Jesus Christ as a result of her godly character with contentment.

She could have chosen to be selfish and abandon her mother in-law after the death of her husband just like the other woman Orpah did. Orpah's name disappeared shortly after that from the book of records in the scriptures, but till today we hear of the name and story of Ruth. As Christians we not only need to pray fervently, but we also need character development. If Godly character is lost, there's not much left to a person. It's character that tells people who you are.

"Know for a fact that "Ability and perseverance can take a person to the height of success, but it is character that would sustain him there". Judas was a disciple of Jesus but among the twelve, he emerged as the "BLACK SHEEP" in the bunch because of character and that was why the devil found the right heart to use in betraying Jesus. May character not debar you from greatness in Jesus name.

PRAYERS FOR THE DAY

*Every power reprogramming my life in order to manipulate my character and destiny, release me in Jesus Name.

*Help me lord to be contented with your blessings in Jesus name.

EXTRA RESOURCES FOR READING
Ruth 1: 1- End., Philippians 2:12-16., Romans 5:4

Giving Thanks for: --

I'm Praying for: --

Devotional Reflections On My Heart Today : ----------------------------------
----

Things I'm Still Struggling With : --

DAY 67
WAKE UP THE MIGHTY MEN
Joel 3:9-12
MEMORY VERSE

Proclaim this among the nations: "Prepare for war! Wake up the mighty men, let all the men of war draw near, let them come up. Joel 3:9 Nkjv

EXPOSITION

The lord is calling on the Men and Women of this generation to wake up from the spiritual slumber that has taken over most of Christendom nowadays. Now, it's all about prosperity and motivational feel good messages everywhere. Spending time with God in aggressive prayers and fasting for long hours has gone cold. The Churches have gone worldly and the world gone churchly. The old-style religion and fire as of old has gone awfully quiet.

Beloved! God is looking for men and women he can depend on in this age. The question for you is this: Can God depend on you for his purpose in this age?. Rev John Knox (1514-1572) prayed "Oh lord "Give me Scotland or I die" but today it is "Give me Money and Fame or I die". As a Christian in this age, given the opportunity to choose between God and worldly fame, which would you choose?

In Mathew 28:18-20, Jesus said "Go into the world and make disciples of me", but how many still believers of today are doing that now. Those who witnessed the great apostolic revivals of yester years would marvel at the level of lukewarmness and Firelessness among believers today. The lord is calling us present day believers, to "wake up as mighty men and women" and fight the good fight of faith. May the lord would help us all in Jesus Name.

PRAYERS FOR THE DAY

*You my Prayer altar, receive deliverance by fire in Jesus name.

* My inner man, receive fresh fire and come alive in Jesus name

EXTRA RESOURCES FOR READING
Revelations 3:1-18., Mathew 5:13-16., Isaiah 40: 28-31.

Giving Thanks for:---

I'm Praying for:---

Devotional Reflections On My Heart Today :------------------------------------
----

Things I'm Still Struggling With :--

-------------------------   ---

DAY 68
WASTED EFFORTS! THE DEVIL'S DESIRE
Luke 5: 5-11
MEMORY VERSE

And Simon answering said unto him, Master, we have toiled all the night, and have taken nothing: nevertheless, at thy word I will let down the net. Luke 5:5 Nkjv

EXPOSITION

Since the beginning of creation, the devil has been waging war against Man. As a matter of fact, it is the desire of the enemy to see to it, that every effort that man puts in on earth in other to achieve success is wasted continually. That's why you'll see someone put money into a business venture, and does everything economically right, but still end up in debt.

That's the joy of the enemy. The Bible commended us to beware of our adversary the devil who prowls about like a roaring lion seeking who he may devour. In the memory verse for today, Peter and his brothers have been fishing all night. They have labored all through and have caught nothing. They have done all the right things professionally to make it work, but yet nothing happened.

Professional fishermen would normally fish at night because that's when fishes come out into the open waters to forage and that's exactly what Peter and his brothers have done, but they could not find anything. However, when Jesus appeared unto him and gave the instructions on what to do, all Peter needed to do was obey, and as he obediently did what he was told, abundance of success followed. Would you listen to Jesus today and see how he'll crown all your efforts with success.?

PRAYERS FOR THE DAY

*Every satanic agenda fashioned against my life in other to waste my efforts, Heavenly Father, waste them in Jesus Name.

* I shall not labor in vain in the name of Jesus.

EXTRA RESOURCES FOR READING
Revelations 3:14-22.,1 Samuel 15:22-24.,1 Corinthians 1: 25-31.

Giving Thanks for:--

I'm Praying for:--

Devotional Reflections On My Heart Today :------------------------------------
----

Things I'm Still Struggling With :--

------------------   --

LISTEN TO GODLY COUNSEL

1 Corinthians 1: 20-29

MEMORY VERSE

Because the foolishness of God is wiser than men, and the weakness of God is stronger than men.1 Corinthians 1:25 Nkjv

EXPOSITION

Believers sometimes struggle with issues in life and because they choose not to listen to divine instructions but instead follow their own human instincts and what their brain tells them, they often fail in those endeavors. This happens most times because the things that God tells them to do, sometimes does not sound rational to the educated human mind.

For example, how do you explain the parting of the red sea by the simple stretching out of Moses Rod to that sea, or the giving a loud shout after going around Jericho city wall seven times and the wall came tumbling down? To the rational educated Christian, that makes no logical sense. That's why the passage above tells us that "the foolishness of God is wiser than the wisdom of Men" and the wisdom of men is foolishness unto God.

Jesus said in Revelations 3: 20 that "behold I stand at the door and knock, if any man hear my voice and opens the door, I would come in and sup with him and he with me". Jesus is calling you today, he doesn't want you and me to continue to struggle without any results if only we would heed his counsel. He doesn't want you to try endlessly without much to show for all the labor you are expending. Come unto him today and he would give your life a new meaning.

PRAYERS FOR THE DAY

*By the power in the blood of Jesus, I shall not labor for the enemy to eat in the name of Jesus.

*Oh lord open my ears to hear your voice clearly when you speak to me and the will power to obey in the name of Jesus.

EXTRA RESOURCES FOR READING

Joshua 6:1-5., Exodus 14:15-31., Proverbs 3:5-6

Giving Thanks for:--

I'm Praying for:--

Devotional Reflections On My Heart Today :----------------------------------
----

Things I'm Still Struggling With :--

DAY 70
GOD HAS A PLAN FOR YOUR LIFE
Jeremiah 29:11-14
MEMORY VERSE

For I know the plans I have for you," declares the LORD, "plans to prosper you and not to harm you, plans to give you hope and a future. Jeremiah 29:11 Niv

EXPOSITION

The plan of God for his children is for them to have peace and joy unlimited in every facet of life. It is his plan for us as Christians to continue to live in dominion every day. However, the enemy has a totally opposite agenda. It is the plan of the enemy to keep people perpetually in slavery and under total ignorance and darkness. Surprisingly, the enemy seems to be gaining grounds in keeping people ignorant because Christians are somewhat lazy to search for the truth.

For this reason, the lord gave man an offer of salvation in which case, we let him into our lives at the time of the new birth, so he can take total control from that point forward. Jesus brings total transformation and liberty of soul and spirit and we are supposed to begin to rule in the spiritual and physical realms. However, some still do not have this revelation knowledge of the power they have in Christ even after the new birth.

Hosea 4:6 says my people are destroyed because they lack knowledge. This knowledge is what the devil tries to make sure that believers get too busy to acquire concerning their situations. But I have good news for you. Whatever situation you might be in now, Jesus is here to take away that burden so that his plan and purpose for your life can come to fulfillment.

PRAYERS FOR THE DAY

*Let the divine agenda of the living God and his purpose begin to manifest in my life in the Name of Jesus.

*Lord I surrender my all to you in the name of Jesus.

EXTRA RESOURCES FOR READING!
Mathew 11:28-30., Hosea 4:4-6

Giving Thanks for:---

I'm Praying for:--

Devotional Reflections On My Heart Today :------------------------------------
----

Things I'm Still Struggling With :---

DAY 71
PROSPERITY IS OF THE LORD
Haggai 2:6-9
MEMORY VERSE
The silver is Mine, and the gold is Mine, 'says the LORD of hosts. Haggai 2:8 Nkjv
EXPOSITION
Every blessing, resources and breakthroughs you could ever desire on the earth is in the hands of our God, because he is the one who has the cattle on a thousand hills. The passage above tells us how wealthy he is and he's making it very clear to us here, so we can stop chasing shadows around and focus on him who is the real deal.

The bible tells us in Phil. 4:19 that "But my God shall supply all my need according to his riches in glory by Christ Jesus". Every need you may ever have on this planet, he is able to supply them, including sound health, housing, cars, clothing, connections, etc. So, why worry yourself when you can pray. He said, "Come unto me all you that labor and are heavy laden and I will give you rest.."

He wants you to live in sound health and prosperity every day of your life. Again, In the book of 3 John 2, he says that "I wish above all things that you prosper and be in health even as your soul prospers.

Jesus is calling on you today, come out of that uncomfortable situation by faith and run unto him and surrender completely to him and your life would never remain the same again. "Remember his thoughts towards you are thoughts of peace", he's always there. He'll supply your needs. May the lord bless and keep you till the end in Jesus Name.
PRAYERS FOR THE DAY
* I break out by fire out of the yoke of financial hardship, and I receive dominion prosperity in the name of Jesus

* Whether the devil likes it or not, I shall prosper in Jesus name.
EXTRA RESOURCES FOR READING!
3 John 2-5., Mathew 11:25-30., Psalms 50:10-12

Giving Thanks for:---

I'm Praying for:---

Devotional Reflections On My Heart Today :----------------------------------
----

Things I'm Still Struggling With :---

------------------------ ---

THE ARM OF FLESH WILL FAIL YOU
Jeremiah 17:5-8
MEMORY VERSE
"Blessed is the man that trusteth in the LORD, and whose hope the LORD is." Jeremiah 17: 7 Kjv
EXPOSITION

God desires for every one of his children to have total trust in him for everything. He doesn't want us to have any other competitor with him because "he is a Jealous God". In the book of Jeremiah 17, God placed a Curse upon whoever looks unto any human being as his source or help. He said "Cursed is the man who trusts in man and makes flesh his strength, whose heart departs from the Lord. For he shall be like a shrub in the desert, and shall not see when good comes, but shall inhabit the parched places in the wilderness, in a salt land which is not inhabited."

This passage indicates that it is a very serious issue before God, and it doesn't look like God is joking about this at all. At times when people trust another human as their source, and they disappoint, such people take it personal and get very angry or upset. What you need to know if that happens to you is that, it means God has not placed your help in the hands of that person though it may seem to you that the person has what it takes to help you.

Psalms 121:1-2 says "I will lift up mine eyes unto the hills, from whence cometh my help. My help cometh from the Lord, which made heaven and earth. Dearly beloved, don't fret, you just change the direction where you look towards for help. If God would not help you, then nobody will. Until help is sent from above, everyone you look to here on earth would disappoint. Beloved! Keep your eyes on the lord.

PRAYERS FOR THE DAY

*Oh lord help me to trust you more and believe you for all I need so I won't be distracted from you in Jesus Name

EXTRA RESOURCES FOR READING

Psalms 121:1-End., Exodus 16:1-36.,1 Kings 17:2-6.

Giving Thanks for:--

I'm Praying for:---

Devotional Reflections On My Heart Today :------------------------------------

----

Things I'm Still Struggling With :--

------------------------   --

DAY 73
HE WILL NOT LET YOU STUMBLE
Psalms 121:1-8
MEMORY VERSE

He will not allow your foot to be moved; He who keeps you will not slumber. Psalms 121:3 Nkjv

EXPOSITION

The lord is your protector, your present help in times of trouble. His ever-watchful eyes is always over your life. Nothing can happen to you unless he permits it and whatever comes your way is always because he wants to bring out the best in it for you for his own glory. He will not suffer your foot to be moved because he that keeps you will not sleep".

The lord would send you the right help for your situation, therefore, it is very important for you to keep your focus on him for everything and in everything. That's when he would organize and package divinely ordained helpers who would never fail you to come your way and settle you in dire situations. Whenever it is as if all hope is lost, and it's as if there's nothing more you can do, that's when he uses an unusual thing or uncommon vessel to sort out the issue.

Remember, the lord is the one "can use an egg to crack a palm kernel just to disgrace a stone". If he can command the Ravens to go and feed Elijah during the drought, if he can use an ordinary widow to feed Elijah during the famine, if he can feed manna to 2 million Jews in the wilderness for 40 years so they don't die of hunger, if he could care for the Israelites in that wilderness for 40 years such that the soles of their sandals did not wither, neither did their clothes wore out? Believe it, He would take care of you. Only trust in him totally.

PRAYERS FOR THE DAY

*Oh lord arise and let every enemy of my full-scale laughter scatter before me in the name of Jesus.

*I shall not be a victim of the trap of the devil in Jesus name.

EXTRA RESOURCES FOR READING

1 Kings 17:1-15., Isaiah 41:10-13., Philippians 4:6-7

Giving Thanks for:---

I'm Praying for:--

Devotional Reflections On My Heart Today :------------------------------------
----

Things I'm Still Struggling With :--

----------------------------------- ---

--- --

DAY 74
HOW DO YOU TREAT YOUR FELLOW MEN?
Mathew 7:12-14.
MEMORY VERSE
Therefore, whatever you want men to do to you, do also to them, for this is the Law and the Prophets. Mathew 7:12 Nkjv

EXPOSITION
There is a natural law that says, "what goes around comes around". The lord told us in Mathew 7:12 that whatsoever we do not want people to do to us, we also should be careful not to do it to them. People often tend to find fault in others especially when they see or perceive that the other person is doing better than them. This often comes either out of jealousy or envy.

It is not uncommon to see people try to bring their fellow man down either directly or cunningly when they see that person attains success earlier than them or when something they so much desire falls into the hand of another person. In places of work, some would go all out to slander and frustrate the efforts of their bosses or co-worker simply because they are eyeing that position or out of sheer hatred.

This also happens in the body of Christ in churches, ministers of God sub planting each other, or doing things that undermines the progress of whichever ministry they are serving, simply because they want the person in charge to look like a failure. In the secular world, friends secretly destroying or undermining each other, while pretending to be sincere to their friendship. Know for a fact that whoever destroys another in other to achieve success would also have destruction awaiting him/her as Sentinel at the post of his Success. Jesus is coming soon.

PRAYERS FOR THE DAY
* Every rage of the enemy against fashioned against my life, be destroyed by the fire of God in the name of Jesus.

*Lord give me the grace to be your true reflection in Jesus name.

EXTRA RESOURCES FOR READING
Luke 6:31-38., Mathew 7:1-12., James 4:11-12.

Giving Thanks for:--

I'm Praying for:---

Devotional Reflections On My Heart Today :-----------------------------------
----

Things I'm Still Struggling With :---

DAY 75
JUDGE NOT, SO YOU WONT BE JUDGED
Mathew 7:1-5
MEMORY VERSE
Judge not, that you be not judged. For with what judgment you judge, you will be judged; and with the measure you use, it will be measured back to you. Mathew 7:1-2 Nkjv

EXPOSITION
How quick do you rush to pass judgement on other people based on unsubstantiated fast circulating information, or rumor you heard from somewhere. Then later when you hear the full story, you then begin to feel terrible about yourself for having rushed to judge and condemn that innocent person after you found out the whole truth.

A lot of people are very guilty of this offense even the so-called Christians. If you pay attention to the word of God in our memory verse today, that commands Christians not to rush to do such if we are to make heaven. This hypocrisy is very common out there, in which people ignore the faults in their own lives and begin to pass judgement on others. Funny enough, many people who do such, often are equally guilty of the same, it's only that their own iniquities have not been exposed yet.

As a Christian, you need to first look at the Beam in your eyes before pointing at the Mote in the other person's eyes. Also know that when you point a finger at the other person, the remaining four fingers points back at you. With the same measure you use for others would it be measured back unto you. Remember! "Do unto others as you would want them to do unto you ". Jesus is coming soon.

PRAYERS FOR THE DAY
* Oh lord help me to follow the leading of the Holy Spirit and my conscience when dealing with others in Jesus Name.

*Lord, help me not to be too judgmental of people in Jesus name.

EXTRA RESOURCES FOR READING
James 4:11-12., Romans 2:1-3., Luke 6:37-42

Giving Thanks for:---

I'm Praying for:---

Devotional Reflections On My Heart Today :----------------------------------
----

Things I'm Still Struggling With :--

------------------------ --

DAY 76
FAILURE IS NOT AN OPTION
Philippians 4:10-13.
MEMORY VERSE
"I can do all things through Christ who strengthens me"
Philippians 4:13 Nkjv.
EXPOSITION
The plan of God is for believers to succeed in everything we lay our hands upon to do. Unfortunately, some people have this failure mentality, always thinking they would fail. Some are even so afraid that because they have failed in the past, they begin to think if they try again, they would fail and for that reason, they don't want to give it a shot anymore. They don't know that "If they fail to try, they are actually trying to fail".

Beloved, the fear of failure is another strategy the enemy wants to use against you to keep you from the success that the lord has planned for you ahead. Since you are a child of God and Jesus the lion of the tribe of Judah dwells in you, then, know it very well that if Jesus cannot fail, then you cannot fail". Failure is not an option for you. He said his plans towards you is for you to prosper. Don't give in to Fear because "Fear has torment "and it is a lie of the enemy.

If you have tried several times before and failed, know that you have just succeeded to find out some ways by which it's not going to work, then, try another method, bring God into the equation and try again. You don't have to stay down because life is all about falling and rising again. Beloved of the lord! Keep trying, don't give up, failure is not an option, don't retreat, don't surrender. You will get there.

PRAYERS FOR THE DAY
* I refuse to be a failure, I refuse to give in to defeat in everything I do, in the Name of Jesus.

* Arrows of failure at the edge of breakthrough, my life is not for you, release me now in the name of Jesus.

EXTRA RESOURCES FOR READING
Jeremiah 29:1-11.,1 John 4:18-20., Philippians 3:10-16.

MY JOURNAL FOR TODAY   /   /20___

Giving Thanks for:--

I'm Praying for:---

Devotional Reflections On My Heart Today :------------------------------------
----

Things I'm Still Struggling With :--

HOW MUCH DO YOU FORGIVE?
Colossians 3:12-17
MEMORY VERSE
"Bearing with one another, and forgiving one another, if anyone has a complaint against another; even as Christ forgave you, so you also must do." Colossians 3:13 Nkjv

EXPOSITION

Beloved! Forgiveness is a virtue, and believe me, not everybody has it. How do you expect God to forgive you when you pray, if you find it hard to forgive others? Some people would rather hold a grudge for years and still come to the house of God to pray. I bet you can now see why answers to prayers are delayed.

The Bible says in the book of Mathew chapter 5 that " anyone who is angry with a brother or sister will be subject to judgment and if you bring your gift to the table and remember your brother has a hurt against you, leave your gift at the altar and quickly go reconcile with your brother and then come back and present your gift at the altar after reconciliation. Then why are people still so unforgiving?

Sometimes, one wonders, what happened to the meaning of the Lord's prayers that we recite "Forgive us our trespasses as we forgive those who trespass against us" Would you rather hold a grudge and have someone live in your head free of charge?. The most interesting part of the story is that often, the person we actually have a grudge against don't even know most times and yet we see such people and we put on a fake smile while living in hatred. May the lord grant you grace to do the right thing in Jesus Name.

PRAYERS FOR THE DAY
*Let the spirit of forgiveness possess me today, in Jesus name.

*Lord help me to not to hold grudges against people who offends me in the name of Jesus.

EXTRA RESOURCES FOR READING
Mathew 6:9-14., Mathew 5:21-26., Ephesians 4:31-31

Giving Thanks for:--

I'm Praying for:---

Devotional Reflections On My Heart Today :-----------------------------------
----

Things I'm Still Struggling With :---

DAY 78
GET RID OF THAT BITTERNESS
Ephesians 4:30-32
MEMORY VERSE

Let all bitterness, wrath, anger, clamor, and evil speaking be put away from you, with all malice. Ephesians 4:31 Nkjv

EXPOSITION

In the passage above, the lord tells us clearly not to exhibit any form of bitterness against anyone. It is very easy for bitterness to creep in, especially when someone around you does negative things to you over and over again, and it's as if such a person is taking your gentleness for foolishness or timidity. Such bitterness often stem from anger that built up over time, and the more you hold unto it, the heavier your heart becomes and that could even result in physical sickness.

Beloved, have you not read what the bible says in 1 John 3:15? that "Whosoever hates his brother is a murderer: and ye know that no murderer has eternal life abiding in him". Even among Husbands and wife's, some hold grudges against each other for years on end and have made up their minds never to forgive and yet they still sleep together on the same bed every night. Just imagine the level of wickedness in the heart of man.

Peter asked Jesus, "Lord, how often should I forgive someone who sins against me? and Jesus replied, seventy times seven times!". This means that matter what it is, we must always forgive and let go. Someone would have to be the Devil's Incarnate to offend you 490 times in a day, meaning that fellow has no other job than getting on your nerves. I pray the lord would give us the grace to obey his word always in Jesus Name.

PRAYERS FOR THE DAY

* Every Root of bitterness and unforgiveness in me, Die in the Name of Jesus.

* Holy ghost fire,, purge my inner man today in Jesus name.

EXTRA RESOURCES FOR READING
Mathew 18:21-35., 1 John3:10-15., 1 Corinthians 13:4-6

Giving Thanks for:--

I'm Praying for:---

Devotional Reflections On My Heart Today :-------------------------------------
----

Things I'm Still Struggling With :---

DAY 79
GO AND LEARN FROM THE ANTS
Proverbs 6:6-11
MEMORY VERSE
"Wisdom is the Principal Thing, therefore get wisdom and in all your getting get understanding" Proverbs 4:7 Nkjv

EXPOSITION

The Bible says Go to the ant, you sluggard; consider its ways and be wise! It has no commander, no overseer or ruler, yet it stores it's provisions in summer and gathers its food at harvest. (Proverbs 6:6-8). Very interesting story and advice we see here in this passage. The Ants are very peculiar creatures that are fascinating to watch while doing their daily routines because they seem to have an idea of time and seasons.

We see these ants very busy, gathering supplies and stocking up their store house in anticipation of the harsh realities of the future. This is called Wisdom, Planning, Organization and Execution. Modern day Christians often live everyday as it comes, without proper strategies for the future and then the enemy begins to win. Humans hardly have regard for Godly wisdom but trusting more in the wisdom of men only to run back to God when their human wisdom fails them as a last resort.

Human beings are the hardest creatures to control on earth, never wanting to submit to authority believing they have free will and wanting to do things as it pleases them but look at these Ants, though they do not seem to have anyone in charge of their activities, they seemingly have a sense of partnership to get the job done. Beloved! Partner with Godly wisdom and be wise.

PRAYERS FOR THE DAY

*The wisdom to do the right things and not to misfire, lord release unto me in the name of Jesus.

*The spirit of understanding from God, possess me in Jesus name.

EXTRA RESOURCES FOR READING
Ecclesiastes 10:1-10., Genesis 8:28-22., 2 kings 5:10-15

Giving Thanks for:--

I'm Praying for:--

Devotional Reflections On My Heart Today :---------------------------------
----

Things I'm Still Struggling With :---

DAY 80
MAKE HAY WHILE THE SUN SHINES
Proverbs 19:19-21
MEMORY VERSE

Listen to counsel and receive instruction, that you may be wise in your latter days. Proverbs 19:20 Nkjv

EXPOSITION

The Bible says, "He that does not work must also not Eat". Therefore, As Christians, let us make hay while the sun is still shining because the time for rest and merriments would still come. Look at the Ants, every day while the weather is fair, these tiny creatures gather into their storerooms, preparing themselves for the harsh realities of the coming weather. In the case of humans, some people would rather sleep and won't lift a finger to do anything but only pray expecting Manna to fall from heaven.

But, here's the reality. What you need to do for yourself, God would not come down and do it for you. In Genesis Chapter 8, the Bible says, "as long as the earth remains, SEEDTIME AND HARVEST shall not cease". Let us as Christians learn these principles and do the right things at the right times and for the right reasons. Only a foolish farmer eats up his/her seed and refuses to plant during the planting season. Therefore, when it is time to Sow, don't hold back.

The word of the lord says, "in the morning sow your seed and in the evening do not hold back because you do not know which one of them would yield the harvest" (Ecclesiastes 11:6). It is wisdom for you to sow only the best seeds because like begets like. You only reap whatever you sow. I pray the lord would help you to take the right steps and follow divine guidance all the way in the Name of Jesus.

PRAYERS FOR THE DAY

* Oh God my father! Order my steps and lead me in the path to follow as I go out every day by day in the name of Jesus.

* I shall not sow in vain in the name of Jesus.

EXTRA RESOURCES FOR READING

1 Peter 2:13-25., Romans 13:1-8., Ephesians 5:15-17

Giving Thanks for:--

I'm Praying for:---

Devotional Reflections On My Heart Today :-----------------------------------
----

Things I'm Still Struggling With :--

DAY 81

A LITTLE SLEEP, A LITTLE SLUMBER

Proverbs 6: 9-12

MEMORY VERSE

A little sleep, a little slumber, A little folding of the hands to sleep, So, shall your poverty come on you like a prowler, And your need like an armed man. Proverbs 6:9-10 Nkjv

EXPOSITION

Once upon a time, there were two brothers who were both curious to know what the future holds in store for them. So one day, both of them went to a Seer to make enquiries and the man told them that one of them came to the world to be rich and would surely be rich, while he said, the other brother has a very bad fortune laying ahead of him in the future and would never amount to anything in life.

Funny enough! the one who received the good prophesy went about telling people that he is born to be rich and famous and very soon his wealth will come and so, all he does is Hope, Pray, Sleeps, and have fun while his brother who received the negative prophesy was determined not to settle for mediocrity. So, he went into the bush and started a farming venture and increased his prayers that God would change his fortune and enlarge his coast just like Jabez did in 1st Chronicles:4

With persistence, hard work, unceasing prayers and dedication, his venture boomed into a very large agricultural plantation and he became really famous and wealthy in no time. His lazy brother ended up being the one in poverty. Beloved!, Prayers would solve a lot of spiritual problems but without hard work and diligence, poverty is lurking around the corner. However, Prayer + Dedication + Hard work = Outstanding Success and Testimonies. Don't just Pray but do it right! Watch and Pray as the scriptures commanded us to do.

PRAYER FOR THE DAY

* Oh Lord! Empower me for success in Jesus name.

EXTRA RESOURCES FOR READING

2 Thessalonians 3:1-10., Proverbs 22:1-29., Romans 12:1-12

Giving Thanks for:---

I'm Praying for:---

Devotional Reflections On My Heart Today :-------------------------------------
----

Things I'm Still Struggling With :---

GOD REWARDS DILIGENCE
Proverbs 22:26-29
MEMORY VERSE

Do you see a man who excels in his work? He will stand before kings; He will not stand before unknown men. Proverbs 22:29 Nkjv

EXPOSITION

Apostle Paul said in 2 Thessalonians 3:10b that "if any would not work, neither should he eat. God honors hard work and diligence backed up with prayers and that's the advantage we have as children of God over the unbelievers, because apart from working hard, we also know how to pray.

Beloved, Our God would not bless an empty hand, it is whatever vocation you have in your hand that God would bless. So, if you want the blessings of God, then, find something to do in the form of a vocation or job. Then when you do all the right things and thereafter asked God to bless your work, then prosperity would show up. Also, if you are praying that God would give you a business of your own, then, do not be sloughtful and nonchalant in someone else's business, otherwise, it'll be hard for God to hand your own business into your hands.

The lord says in Luke 16:12 that "And if you have not been faithful in what is another man's, who will give you what is your own? This is because, whatever you do in another man's business is what you'll do in yours. We need to learn diligence and dedication in whatever we do as children of God. Then, we'll see him moving in our affairs and we'll have a good reward for our labor.

PRAYERS FOR THE DAY

*Arrows of failure in my life, jump out and die in Jesus name.

*The anointing and grace to excel, in whatever I lay my hands upon to do, fall upon me in the name of Jesus.

EXTRA RESOURCES FOR READING
Luke 16:9-12., Proverbs 13:1-4., Proverbs 21:1-5

Giving Thanks for:--

I'm Praying for:--

Devotional Reflections On My Heart Today :----------------------------------
----

Things I'm Still Struggling With :---

BREAK UP YOUR FALLOW GROUND
Jeremiah 4:2-4
MEMORY VERSE
"For thus saith the Lord to the men of Judah and Jerusalem, Break up your fallow ground, and sow not among thorns." Jeremiah 4:3 Nkjv
EXPOSITION
A fallow ground is a land on which the farmer has not planted any crop for a long time and is left to be overgrown with weeds & thorns in other for that land to recover. This is the state of the heart of man. It is filled with different kinds of evil thoughts, and various vices.

However, the lord is telling us that in other for us to be a tool for righteousness which the lord could use, we need to break into these areas and clear all these thorns so that the word of the lord may richly grow upon the cleared fertile ground in us. Break off your evil ways, repent of your sins, cease to do evil, and then the good seed of the word will have room to grow and bear fruit unto righteousness in your life.. Colossians 3:16a says Let the word of Christ dwell in you richly.

In Hosea 10:12, the Bible commands us to sow our seeds in righteousness so that we may reap in accord with loving kindness because Jesus is coming back for a bride (church) that is without spot and blemish. Every fallow ground that's not occupied has the potential of being taken over by the enemy. Remember, "an idle mind is the devil's workshop." I pray the lord would strengthen us to discipline ourselves and to wholly submit ourselves to be a living sanctuary for him to dwell in Jesus Name.

PRAYERS FOR THE DAY
* Arrows of failure in my life, jump out and die in Jesus name.

* I repossess every fallow ground of my life and I command them to begin yielding their increase unto me in the name of Jesus.
EXTRA RESOURCES FOR READING
Hosea 10:1-12., Colossians3:1-16., Mathew13:1-23.

Giving Thanks for:---

I'm Praying for:--

Devotional Reflections On My Heart Today :--

Things I'm Still Struggling With :---

DAY 84
ACCORDING TO YOUR FAITH
Mathew 9: 18-29
MEMORY VERSE

But without faith it is impossible to please him: for he that cometh to God must believe that he is, and that he is a rewarder of them that diligently seek him. Hebrews 11:6 Nkjv

EXPOSITION

In the book of Mathew chapter 9, Jesus attended to three cases demonstrating what faith can do. The first was the daughter of a certain ruler who was raised from the dead because of the man's unusual faith. The second was the woman with the issue of blood and the third were the two blind men who didn't give up until Jesus attended to them. Jesus either said "Their faith has made them whole or be it unto them according to their faith, except the ruler who professed his faith in Jesus with his mouth.

Beloved, these are the kinds of faith, trust and confidence that our lord expects us to have in him. He said if you would have faith like a Mustard seed, we would change even the seemingly impossible. All it takes to get things done with the lord is just a little faith. I mean a very tiny amount of faith and we'll begin to see things get done supernaturally in our lives and we'll begin a life of dominion on earth.

The Mustard seed is the tiniest of all seeds but inside that tiny seed is the potential to become the largest of all trees once it gets into the ground and have a little taste of water. That Mustard seed is the faith and the water it needs to sprout and germinate is the power of God. These two only needs to make contact in order for things to begin to fall in place miraculously. Receive grace to believe in Jesus name.

PRAYERS FOR THE DAY

* By the power in the blood of Jesus, I command every seed of faithlessness in me to die in the Name of Jesus.

* Lord empower me to trust in you always in the name of Jesus.

EXTRA RESOURCES FOR READING
Mathew 17:14-21., Luke 17: 1-6

Giving Thanks for:--

I'm Praying for:--

Devotional Reflections On My Heart Today :--

Things I'm Still Struggling With :---

--------------------   --

DAY 85
MAKE GOD YOUR ONE AND ONLY PLAN
Isaiah 42:5-9
MEMORY VERSE
I am the Lord, that is My name; And My glory I will not give to another, Nor My praise to carved images. Isaiah 42:8 Nkjv

EXPOSITION

Isn't it funny enough that people would get up and dress up and head to church with a whole load of requests in their mind and get down on their knees and talk to God about those requests, but yet don't believe in the one they are talking to enough to get that request done for them? Instead, they already have a back-up plan somewhere at the back of their mind, just in case God fails to answer on time, they quickly run to their back up plan.

This is faith like that of the doubting Thomas. No wonder things don't happen. Just wait a minute! Before you begin to put your back up plan together, so you don't waste your time. The Bible says Our God is a jealous God and his glory he would not share with any man.

Instead of him to share his glory with your back up plan, he would rather wait until you are ready to fully trust and fully dependent on him like the Woman with the 12 years issue of blood who was already out of options and had no other choice but to run to the master or like the Ruler mentioned in Mathew chapter 9 whose daughter was dead and all hopes was lost for him. Remember "without faith it's impossible to please God". The lord needs and demands our total and complete trust in him. All things are possible to them that believe.

PRAYERS FOR THE DAY

* Oh lord release unto me the grace I need to trust you completely in every situation in the name of Jesus.

* Lord I believe you are able to get things done for me, I know you'll make things beautiful for me in your own time in Jesus name.

EXTRA RESOURCES FOR READING
Hebrews 11:1-7., Isaiah 42:1-9

Giving Thanks for:--

I'm Praying for:--

Devotional Reflections On My Heart Today :----------------------------------
----

Things I'm Still Struggling With :--

------------------   --

DAY 86
OBSTACLES ARE UNAVOIDABLE
Proverbs 3: 5-6
MEMORY VERSE

These things I have spoken to you, that in Me you may have peace. In the world you will have tribulation; but be of good cheer, I have overcome the world." John 16:33 Nkjv

EXPOSITION

In life, obstacles are totally unavoidable, and they can come as tragedies, financial meltdowns, hindrances, rejection etc. which could make us wonder if God has abandoned us. Know that no trial has come upon you that is new to man, but God would not allow us to be tried beyond what our strength can carry, but he is able to make a way of escape for us.

Life is not always going to be smooth, so if you think you are the only one experiencing setbacks or obstacles, then think again, because God has not promised Christians a stress-free life. He wants to make our setbacks to become our steppingstones to elevation. The Bible says, consider it pure joy, my brothers and sisters, whenever you face trials of many kinds, because you know that the testing of your faith produces perseverance (James 1:2-4) to make us mature and complete.

The stumbling blocks we face on our road to success would not be as bad as they look if we focus on the lord. Because what we call satanic roadblocks or setbacks are just little tests the lord allowed in our lives in order to prepare us for greater assignments ahead or to just train us on a few simple facts of life.

PRAYERS FOR THE DAY

* Every satanic obstacle on the way to my promotion, Holy Ghost uproot them in the Name of Jesus

*Oh Lord, help me not to fail you during my time of testing in the name of Jesus.

EXTRA RESOURCES FOR READING

1 Peter 5:7., Mathew 6:25-27., James 1:12-14., Isaiah 41:13

Giving Thanks for:--

I'm Praying for:--

Devotional Reflections On My Heart Today :----------------------------------
----

Things I'm Still Struggling With :--

--------------------- --

-- --

DAY 87
DON'T TURN BACK
Luke 9:59-62
MEMORY VERSE

But Jesus said to him, "No one, having put his hand to the plow, and looking back, is fit for the kingdom of God."
Luke 9:62 Nkjv

EXPOSITION

Ok! You read it right! Don't turn back!!! There are people today among believers who have become experts at quitting. Just a little bit of roadblock or challenge on the way and Boom! they quit. Yet the same people would complain about how things are not moving as fast for them or things are not working the way it should be.

Jesus said in our memory verse above, there's no one who puts his hands on the plow and looks back that's fit for the kingdom of God. In the book of Exodus, the children of Israel after the mighty deliverance through the Red Sea complained against the lord and contemplated going back to Egypt. Little did they know that God was busy doing things and perfecting everything that concerns them. If only people know how close they are to their breakthroughs before turning back, they'll hang on a little longer.

Whatever goal or aspirations you might be pursuing now, and it seems as if it's not working out, it's not time yet to back off. You are only learning some lessons that you need for the future in the "School of Hard Knocks. If Thomas Edison had given up and turned back after failing over and over again, he wouldn't have got it right. Don't turn back, pursue those dreams and you'll get there if you persist.

PRAYERS FOR THE DAY

* Every power that wants me to give up at the edge of my breakthrough release me in the Name of Jesus.

*I shall succeed, I shall excel in my endeavors in Jesus name.

EXTRA RESOURCES FOR READING
Isaiah 41:8-10., Joshua 1: 9-11., Philippians 4:11-13

Giving Thanks for: ---

I'm Praying for: ---

Devotional Reflections On My Heart Today : ---

Things I'm Still Struggling With : --

DAY 88
DIVINE VISITATION
Luke 19:1-9
MEMORY VERSE

And when Jesus came to the place, He looked up and saw him, and said to him, "Zacchaeus, make haste and come down, for today I must stay at your house. Luke 19:5 Nkjv

EXPOSITION

The visitation of God does not happen in the life of people but on the day when God decides to visit someone, he doesn't always announce it and because of this some have missed their own day of visitation because they were not prepared for it, just like the five foolish virgins who were not ready for their day of visitation in Mathew 25.

The bible commands us in Mathew 24:42 to watch and pray because we do not know the hour when the lord would come. In today's memory verse above, Zacchaeus who was a Tax collector, a chief of sinners of his generation, who was not qualified to even have Jesus enter into his house by the standards of that age had that divine encounter because he was desperate and also was in the right place at the right time .That day turned to his day of transformation and divine encounter.

The day a king or President singles you out and visits you with favor, that day your life cannot remain the same again. That's an earthly king visiting you, how much more if the maker of the universe visits you. Divine visitation is not about your qualification or personal ability, but it's divine grace and mercy. May you receive a divine encounter today in the name of Jesus.

PRAYERS FOR THE DAY

* I shall not miss my day of divine visitation and transformation in the Name of Jesus.

*Oh lord visit me with favor today in the name of Jesus.

EXTRA RESOURCES FOR READING

1 Chronicles 13:9-14., 1 Kings 17:7-16., Genesis 21:1-3

Giving Thanks for:--

I'm Praying for:--

Devotional Reflections On My Heart Today :----------------------------------
----

Things I'm Still Struggling With :---

------------------   --

DAY 89
UNIVERSAL CURRENCY
Romans 3:21-26
MEMORY VERSE
"For all have sinned and fall short of the glory of God, being justified freely by His grace through the redemption that is in Christ Jesus" Romans 3:23-24 Nkjv

EXPOSITION
The currency of any Kingdom or Nation is the universally acceptable means of exchange in that Society. Which means whatever you want to obtain or achieve in that society, you must have that currency to be able to get it done. So, whoever does not have that currency in his possession in that society would be practically helpless.

Such is the case in the kingdom of God. Jesus came and died for us on the cross of Calvary, exchanging his life of righteousness for our own life of sin as final and full payment for our transgressions either in the past, present, or future, giving us eternal life and thereby releasing unto us "GRACE" as the Universal currency that we can use as long as we are on the face of this earth because of his great love for us miserable sinners.

This unmerited favor of God called grace is what gives us the boldness to come before God even when we sin and ask for mercy sincerely and he grants that mercy unto us. By grace we have been saved according to the love which Christ bestowed on us. This grace is what shields us from the anger of God. It is what opens doors which sin and the enemy has shut against you. Receive grace for exploits and dominion in Jesus Name.

PRAYERS FOR THE DAY
*Uncommon grace from the throne of God, fall upon my life in the Name of Jesus.

*The mercy of God that overrides every judgement of man, let it be released unto me today in the name of Jesus.

EXTRA RESOURCES FOR READING
Ephesians 2:1-13., Titus 2:11-12., Hebrews 4:14-16

Giving Thanks for:--

I'm Praying for:---

Devotional Reflections On My Heart Today :---------------------------------------
----

Things I'm Still Struggling With :---

DAY 90
IT IS FINISHED
John 19: 28-30
MEMORY VERSE
For this reason, the gospel was preached even to those who are now dead, so that they might be judged according to human standards in regard to the body but live according to God in regard to the spirit. 1 Peter 4:6 Nkjv

EXPOSITION
Let's take a laborer who has worked long hours in the sun. It's only natural for that person to be thirsty because he would naturally be exhausted due to body electrolytes that would have been lost in the hot sun. Likewise, Jesus labored under the weight of our sins on the cross and on the long arduous journey to Calvary, he therefore made known his desire for water saying, "I thirst".

Jesus was thirsty on the cross, so you would no longer thirst for anything, because he bore it all. He said whosoever is thirsty may come unto me, and I would give unto him the living water (John 7:37-39). After completing the work of redemption, he said "it is finished", meaning the final payment for your debts, sicknesses, trials, tribulations, heart aches, worries, losses, hardships, tragedies, sorrows and pain has been paid in full.

Therefore, as a child of God, learn to use this knowledge and authority to face every challenge that comes your way and speak directly unto such situations telling such situations directly, that Jesus has settled this. Therefore, the devil has no right to lay his ugly hands on you again. May the lord would give us insight and boldness to apply this knowledge into our daily lives in Jesus Name. Jesus paid it all.

PRAYERS FOR THE DAY
* Every legal ground the enemy has over my life, become sinking sand by the power and authority in the name of Jesus.

*Every Yoke of Iniquity in my life, Break by Fire in name Jesus

EXTRA RESOURCES FOR READING
1 Peter 1:18-19., Isaiah 53:1-12., John19:1-42

Giving Thanks for:--

I'm Praying for:--

Devotional Reflections On My Heart Today :-------------------------------------
----

Things I'm Still Struggling With :--

APPENDIX
BIBLE TRANSLATIONS

CEV: Contemporary English Version
New York: American Bible Society. (1995)

ESV: English Standard Version
Illinois: Crossway Bibles of Wheaton. (2008)

KJV: Holman King James Version Study Bible
Nashville, Tennessee: Holman Bible Publishers. (2012)

NASB: New American Standard Bible
Anaheim, CA: Foundation Press. (1973)

NIV: New International Version
Colorado Springs: Biblica; Formerly International Bible Society. (1978)

NKJV: New King James Version
Nashville: Nelson. (1982)

VISION **T**ITLES
PUBLISHING
OWINGS MILLS, MARYLAND 21117 USA

Lightning Source UK Ltd.
Milton Keynes UK
UKHW041545051022
409889UK00013B/294